First printed January 2020

This edition printed October 2021 by The Happy Brain Co Ltd

Company registered in England and Wales No 13470114

www.thehappybrainco.com

Because of the dynamic nature of the Internet, any web addresses or links contained in this book may have changed since publication and may no longer be valid. The views expressed in this work are solely those of the author and do not necessarily reflect the views of the publisher, and the publisher hereby disclaims any responsibility for them.

ISBN: 978-1-7399720-0-4

the happy brain co.

www.thehappybrainco.com

Praise for Happy Brain™

This is a delightful book. Kay Cooke does what NLP should be, keeping it powerful and simple. Read this book and learn to make your life simple and more powerful in a delightful way!
Dr. Richard Bandler, co-founder of Neuro Linguistic Programming

This is a remarkable book. Grounded in science and backed by years of experience, Kay Cooke has taken complex ideas and made them accessible and easy to understand. More than this, it gives every parent, carer, teacher or coach beguilingly simple processes to support children in their journey through life's challenges.
There has been a concerning move towards a medicalisation of childhood, where labels and 'syndromes' are used to 'explain' behaviour, sadly without any meaningful helping or coping strategies. In this book, Kay Cooke provides a positive and effective alternative. Here you learn what is actually going on with a child and learn effective strategies to help them to overcome challenges. More than this, it gives you the tools to enable children in your care to thrive and flourish as they grow and learn. I highly recommend you read this book and make it a tool in your everyday life. You may even find that you learn how to have a Happy Brain™ too!
Kate Benson, Director of Education for the Society of NLP

Any parent, carer, teacher, or professional working with children with emotional, psychological or behavioural difficulties simply must read this book. Not to do so serves a great disservice to these children. Ideally, the book will help teachers, parents and carers to prevent such problems occurring. When this is not possible, it will help everyone quickly and easily resolve difficulties, leading to a rapid return to good mental health and happy children who enjoy learning and life.
Dr Louise Golightly, MB,BS., MRCPsych, Consultant Psychiatrist

This book is a thorough and eloquent guide to how people, particularly children, learn best. Anyone who follows the advice and methods in this book will help children to access the skills and resources they have to learn effectively. The children will also learn to nurture their emotional health towards the flexibility necessary to live full and rewarding adult lives in a caring society in future. I would strongly urge anyone who recognises the wisdom within these pages to practise and master the attitudes and techniques described.
Dr Mark E W Chambers. M.B., Ch.B., FRCGP

This is an amazing book - clear, lively, readable and full of fascinating facts, procedures and appraisals. What it's about and who it's for are best summed up for me by the author, who writes: "I set out to try to persuade teachers and parents that seemingly low-key - yet enormously impactful - play activities would build more resourceful and resilient young minds.
Elaine Perry, Emeritus Professor, Neurochemical Pathology, Newcastle University

Kay brings enormous passion to starting the process of giving all children a healthier mindset in their learning environment. She has left me with an array of tools that have been incredibly useful to aid the development of pupils' self-awareness, resilience and confidence. In addition, she has always been willing to advise me on further progress as my understanding of these power tools deepens.
Sarah Piper, teacher

This is a brilliant, multi-lightbulb-flashing experience; a fantastically engaging, thought-provoking, enlightening and inspiring model. A wonderful introduction to a thrilling new discipline with which I can enhance every area of my life. I look forward to learning all there is to know - and more - about Happy Brain™.
Jane, parent

Parenting any child is a joy, a challenge and a huge responsibility all at once. How can we, as parents, educators and the community as a whole, ensure that we have done our best to give them the life they deserve? How can we help to prevent failures and falls; ensure they are strong and resilient; and there is no such thing as barriers to learning? This model resonates with the brain training I do with neurofeedback, as it aims to form better brain pathways as a means to ensure learning and thriving with no barriers and language pollution. Addressing basic needs and building on feeling listened to and secure – this is how we teach brain to thrive. As a parent and a coach, I strongly believe that Happy Brain™ will equip anyone with techniques that make them a much better parent, teacher, coach or therapist.
Tatiana Stewart, optimal brain training and performance coach

I'm very excited to see something in action allowing people to take away simple skills that have been distilled from incredible complexity. And one of the key learnings for me is that prevention happens at every stage in life, because there's always another stage. And whether you're a child, a grandparent, parent or somewhere in-between, you're still around children and you have the ability to influence. So why not do it in a really positive way?
Orlando Zucchetto, NLP trainer

As a holistic therapist, mother and human being, Happy Brain™ offers numerous strategies and ideas that are useful both on a personal and professional level. Highly recommended for all!
Laura Lee, holistic therapist

I have trained with Kay over several years and she is now my go-to person for anything related to developing self. Her knowledge is outstanding and her style of delivery is personal, specific and fun. Happy Brain™ has the potential to bring so much to the world of wellbeing and thriving. It has given me further insight into where clients process their responses, which is helpful in directing their brain towards a more helpful pattern. Even being able to 'explain' the brain in this accessible way is helpful to my clients.
Tracey Hutchinson, performance coach

My son had been badly bullied and was suffering from flashbacks and constant mental trauma. I was desperate for help. Within one Happy Brain™ session you lifted the weight from his shoulders and helped him to eliminate the pain and the trauma from the memories which had tortured him. I am forever grateful - you gave me my happy, fun-loving son back.
Janice, parent

Kay is a skillful, passionate person, teaching from her personal experience and excited to show you the way. I recommend Happy Brain™ for parents, teachers and caregivers as it helps our kids to express themselves while playing and lead them to bloom. I can positively say that Happy Brain™ has made me a better mother and made my kids happier. Thank you.
Marie-Therese, parent

Happy Brain™ has exceeded my expectations of using NLP models in a more appropriate way for working with children.
Tina Taylor, NLP Master Trainer, coach, author

Happy Brain™ gives us a multi-dimensional framework for understanding how best to teach children and young people how to thrive. It's so refreshing to have a model that brings together, in simple, playful and clear approaches, everything you need to develop resilience in those you love, support and work with. Kay's holistic approach to wellbeing and her many years of learning and teaching are brought to you in this wonderfully positive, practical and insightful book. Enjoy the read, and enjoy the learning as you develop and share the wisdom within.
Julie Olsson, NLP Trainer, teacher, learning coach

Kay has really helped us as a whole family. She has given us a new perspective on parenting and equipped us with strategies to help defuse situations where our son's emotions were getting out of control. She also worked closely with our son to help him gain control over his emotions. We have gained confidence in parenting and learned to trust and believe in our son again.
Angie and Rob, parents

happybrain
next-generation thinking

USING PLAY, CREATIVITY AND NLP TO SUPERCHARGE YOUR CHILD'S THRIVE DRIVE

Kay Cooke

For our children

Happy Brain™: NEXT-GENERATION THINKING

PUTTING OUR CHILDREN'S EMOTIONAL RESILIENCE AND MENTAL HEALTH IN OUR HANDS

Happy Brain™ is the result of decades of work by parent, coach, teacher and therapist Kay Cooke. Her experience in helping children and young people to build Thrive skills, and her special interest in using play and creativity to build emotional resilience and good mental health, are the essence of this book.

This is a manual for everyone inspired to make positive changes in the way they think, the way they interact with children and young people, and the means by which they help children and young people to live happier, healthier lives. With this book, the tools for emotional resilience and mental health are in your hands.

Contents

Foreword xvi
Preface... xvii
Introduction... xviii

About   i. About mental health.. xx
                   ii. About Happy Brain™ - the original project xxii
                   iii. About this book xxv

Chapter One   All models are useful 1

Chapter Two   The Principle of Simplicity 7

Chapter Three The Principle of Resilience..39

Chapter Four   i. When the lights are on, but no one's home 70
                   ii. The Principle of Clarity... 71

Chapter Five   The magic ingredient..95

Chapter Six   Motivation..107

Chapter Seven Case studies 115

                   Afterword 137
                   Useful references.. 138
                   Further reading.. 140

Editor: **Jane Pikett**
Design & layout: **Stuart Blackie**
Original drawings: **Emily Allinson**
Illustrations: **Laura Lee**
www.thehappybrainco.com

"Tell it to me like I'm a five-year-old,
because when you can, then you truly know it"

JOHN LA VALLE

PRESIDENT OF THE SOCIETY OF NLP™

Foreword

This is an amazing book - clear, lively, readable and full of fascinating facts, procedures and appraisals. What it's about and who it's for are best summed up for me by the author, who writes: "*I set out to try to persuade teachers and parents that seemingly low-key, yet enormously impactful, play activities would build more resourceful and resilient young minds.*"

Kay Cooke has great enthusiasm, conveying complex concepts such as how the human brain works in an engaging and – the bit I do know about – accurate and up-to-date way.

As a professional psychotherapist, she describes procedures (play activities), and how and why they work so vividly that I found myself, a neuroscientist as opposed to a psychologist, carried away and trying out techniques. Balloon breathing certainly seems to work as a de-stressor for me.

As a neuroscientist, my programmed response to new therapies of any kind is to demand objective evidence; something like a placebo-controlled trial that depends on an approved experimental design and assessment by observers independent of the procedures. And NLP, one of the psychotherapeutic procedures that lies behind Kay's new model, has only limited supporting evidence of that kind.

But however hard we try, we can't take the subject out of the equation; just look at how the neuroscience of consciousness still hits rocks as it tries and fails to translate some subjective experiences (is the red I see the same colour as the red you see?) to particular brain cells or neural networks. So, we old-school scientists have to take subjective evidence such as is presented in this book seriously.

Kay's observations, kids' responses, parental and other assessors' reports are all evidence that standard efficacy and safety criteria are fulfilled. And even if it were possible to design a placebo-controlled trial of some of Kay's procedures, we are faced with some extraordinary facts about the placebo. Not only does the expectation of being in a trial of a new technique, not knowing if you are in the test or placebo group, lead to positive outcomes, but there's new evidence that some people respond positively even knowing they're on a placebo!

More than that, for any scientist willing to look at evidence on the effect of intention (evidence, as objective as it can be, if not yet high-profile) it's clear that just holding the intention to heal in mind can work for some people (healers and patients). So subjective is part of any equation, and in Happy Brain™ it's all backed by fascinating 'facts': how when brain cells fire together they form stronger connections tells us why out-of-sync brainwaves may be bad for you.

I may have been referring less to the specific contents of the book and more to the principles of deciding what to take seriously. But the objective-subjective evidence debate is important, especially for potential readers in mainstream medical practice. So, I would say to them and to my science colleagues, read this book, see how some of these novel techniques might be relevant to you or your work.

Happy Brain™ may help a lot of youngsters in need (treatment), and others not yet in need (protection). This generation of kids, faced with so many choices and challenges, must not end up fitting DSM diagnostic criteria for anxiety or depression when they could be helped not only to avoid that (survive), but also thrive to create an (even) better world.

Elaine Perry, Emeritus Professor
Neurochemical Pathology, Newcastle University
November 2019

Preface

I've always been fascinated by the pursuit of health and happiness - for myself and for others. This has emerged through a lifetime of personal and professional development, and various career paths including sports coaching, high school teaching, college lecturing, health promotion, and mentoring others as an award-winning entrepreneur in the creative industries.

There were tricky times along the way; including as a single mum experiencing the ravages of mental health problems while trying to navigate a path through a system that labelled a couple of my kids as 'different' to their peers.

A significant life event in 2005 prompted me to train in Neuro Linguistic Programming (NLP) - the practice of re-organising your thinking, feeling, language and behaviour to produce more rewarding results.

Through this study, I discovered the Bandler Technologies® of NLP co-founder Richard Bandler. These provided me with a new way to restructure life for myself and my family, building the future I now love; teaching models of health, happiness and wellbeing.

Today, I'm a volunteer Samaritan and proud mum to five grown-up children. I travel internationally as a Society of NLP™ trainer and I'm qualified in many holistic systems, all of which support my work as a Mind Coach, Brain Trainer and Holistic Therapist.

Helping people of all ages brings me into contact with common problems such as anxieties, fears, phobias, bullying, performance anxiety, relationship difficulties, school pressure, learning difficulties, depression, labels (ADHD, dyspraxia, ASD, dyslexia etc.), trauma, bereavement, suicidal feelings and self-harm. My therapy work is interventional, while my coaching and training focuses on the preventative, helping people to build models of resilience that prevent future problems.

When I'm working with kids, I call our sessions 'mind coaching'. After all, sports coaching is an everyday thing, so why not mind coaching? Working with children, young adults and families who are struggling is my favourite work - perhaps because I understand these problems from the inside out, and definitely because building resilience within young people is the best hope for all our futures. This book will help you to develop simple tools to do that too; welcome to Happy Brain™, and thank you for reading.

Kay Cooke November 2019

Introduction

This book is a thorough and eloquent guide to how people, particularly children, learn best. It is powerful and easy to read, the learning points clearly explained and the case studies lucidly illustrating the principles and techniques in action. It is thoroughly researched and there is an excellent reference section that invites the interested reader to explore further.

The author's background is in teaching at all ages, coaching, mentoring and holistic therapy. She is also a very experienced practitioner and trainer of Neuro Linguistic Programming (NLP), a Samaritan and a mother. This eclectic mix is evident throughout the book, which is a compelling and inspiring primer of how learning can be achieved and optimised, particularly with children and even in quite adverse circumstances.

The techniques that emerge through the book are informed and supported by Kay's understanding and knowledge in the fields of contemporary neuroscience, psychology and education. The principles underlying the techniques are discussed and useful models for applying them are progressively developed.

We know that emotional and psychological suffering in adult life is often preceded by missed opportunities in learning and the appropriate processing of childhood experiences at the time they occur. This book thoroughly addresses these matters. Issues explored include the prevention of mental illness by timely intervention in childhood, the building of resilience skills, and the use of the resourcefulness of children and their amazing capacity for imagination and creativity.

The children already have the answers. They are their own textbook. This book raises the reader's awareness of how to access and elicit the intuitive wisdom of the child and help him or her to harness their own resources to their own best ends. These are essential life-skills.

After a clear introduction, Kay explains the rationale of the book and why this work is so important for our children's futures. Subsequent chapters develop the models underpinning her approach and explain their application with numerous examples and illustrations. The importance of awareness and constant, accurate calibration of the mental state and processing of the child and the interventionist, both conscious and unconscious, are constantly stressed.

There are many techniques to help identify and calm the stressed brain at different levels, and then put it to work creatively in learning using the principles of Simplicity, Resilience and Clarity as beacons. The chapter on identifying and meeting needs binds the approach together by giving a clear focus for the rest of the work.

This book is of value to parents, teachers, coaches and all professionals whose work brings them into contact with children. A knowledge of NLP is not required to fully access the wisdom and advice in its pages, but anyone with a knowledge of NLP will be able to identify how the attitudes and practices of NLP have informed this work.

The examples Kay uses to illustrate her techniques demonstrate the versatility of her approach and her ability to find her way past labels to compassionately nurture and develop the young people behind them. I found the account of helping 'Adrian' in Chapter 7 particularly moving and demonstrative of the gentle power of her approach.

Anyone who follows the advice and methods in this book will be helping children to access the skills and resources they have to learn effectively. Children will also learn to nurture their emotional health towards the flexibility necessary to live full and rewarding adult lives in a caring society in future.

This book is just the start. Reading is no substitute for practical experience. Nothing is learned until it is felt in the bone. I would strongly urge anyone who recognises the wisdom within these pages to practise and master the attitudes and techniques described. I would particularly encourage people to attend the practical courses Kay runs in order to gain personal experience of these techniques in action. Kay has achieved the great feat of modelling her own excellence in these pages. She walks the walk, and that is what makes this book a compelling, motivating and convincing read - a worthy addition to the resource base for effective learning.

Dr. Mark E W Chambers. M.B., Ch.B., FRCGP
November 2019

About

i. About mental health

In my work as a therapist, coach, teacher, and volunteer Samaritan, I see the current mental health paradigm producing devastating results.

Self-harm and suicides draw media attention, but still millions of adults are trapped in mental prisons. It seems that human brains are ill-equipped to deal with the complexities of the system in which we try to live.

According to the UK Mental Health Foundation (NICE Common Mental Health Disorders 2011): "Mixed anxiety and depression is the most common mental disorder in Britain, estimated to cause one fifth of days lost from work."

If one adult in six (another UK Mental Health Foundation statistic from the Adult Psychiatric Morbidity Survey 2014) has suffered a common mental health disorder, you don't have to look far to see this playing out.

According to the UK Health & Safety Executive's Labour Force Survey in March 2019: "In 2016/17, 526,000 workers were suffering from stress, depression or anxiety (new or long-standing) and 12.5 million working days were lost as a result of this."

Adult mental health problems are frequently traced back to difficulties in childhood, in particular adverse childhood events (ACEs). Interestingly, not all children who experience ACEs go on to develop problems and it seems that the level of childhood 'resilience', i.e., **mental and emotional flexibility, is key to the child's ability to deal with life's ongoing experiences.**

My personal mission and sense of purpose comes from my Happy Brain™ work, which equips children, their parents, teachers and caregivers with skills to deal with whatever life events, whirlwinds and traumas they may face.

A UK Children's Society report in 2008 said: "10% of children and young people have a diagnosable mental health problem and 70% of those have not had appropriate intervention at a sufficiently early age."

And, according to a recent NASUWT (UK Teachers' Union) survey, 96% of teachers believe they come into contact with pupils who are experiencing mental health issues. Of these, 92% say pupils are exhibiting anxiety or panic attacks, 80% say they have experience of pupils suffering depression and 67% encounter pupils exhibiting symptoms of self-harm.

"Teachers have never before had to deal with such a complex range of pupil welfare issues as they do today... The pressure on teachers and head teachers is enormous and is putting at risk their own mental and physical health and wellbeing," said Chris Keates, General Secretary NASUWT in The Daily Telegraph (April 2018)

Why wait for intervention? Let's teach children robust skills that nurture their mental health, ahead of time. It's not fair to simply 'talk about' mental health; we have to provide young people with a roadmap and a toolkit to effect positive change.

My ambition is to contribute to a society and an education system that builds sustainable mental, emotional and physical (whole child) wellbeing. That is at the heart of this book.

ii. About Happy Brain™
– the original project

Happy Brain™ was created in 2010 as a consultancy project funded by the UK Arts Council. My brief was to creatively inspire teachers to help young people to **overcome barriers to learning.**

Since I already had a thriving coaching/therapy practice and a creative toolkit for helping children to learn about themselves and learn how to learn, I knew that working in the classroom with children would be the easiest part of this project.

However, children don't live in isolation, and their wider system has a massive influence on how and what they learn. **So I set out to try to persuade teachers and parents that seemingly low-key - yet enormously impactful - play activities would build more resourceful and resilient young minds capable of good-quality learning.**

I began to design a model that would encourage both adults and children to learn how their brains work best. Early inspiration for the delivery style came partly from my 1990s work as a Happy Heart tutor delivering the UK Health Education Authority's Look After Your Heart Look After Yourself initiative. That was a schools' programme with an educational training manual and a pack of wipe-clean Happy Heart activity cards.

Also, remembering my own preceding decades as a parent, teacher and children's coach helped me to respect a central tenet of Neuro Linguistic Programming (NLP), the applied psychology which informs my work, which says: *'Everyone is doing the best they can with the resources available'.*

I found myself regularly reflecting upon a question - *'what was it I needed to know back then, that I know now?'* Finding those answers helped me to find my voice and direct the project.

For the task of meeting the original project brief, which was *overcoming barriers to learning,* I asked myself four questions:

1. **What do they mean by 'learning'?**
   The answer was 'learning the national (educational) curriculum'.
2. **Since humans are naturally exquisite learning machines, what are children learning instead of the curriculum and why?**
   The answer was 'learning how to Survive daily (subjective) Stresses'.

3. **What do children need to re-direct their attention and engagement to learning the curriculum?**

   The answer was 'adults with understanding of how a brain makes everyday decisions based on non-logical Survival mechanisms'.

4. **What do teachers/adults need to know/do differently?**

   The answer was a coherent framework and model of simplicity. NLP would provide a superb foundation for this.

Finding these answers helped me to conceptualise a model that would hopefully speak volumes to teachers and pupils.

What quickly became apparent was that kids in class who were 'Stressed' (the term 'Stress' can mean many things, as we will explore later), were diverting their attention away from the educational system's needs and towards behaviours more akin to Survival needs.

Many were regularly triggering Survival-like reactions inside their brains that prevented them and their peers from flourishing. It's not that kids are truly in Survival mode, it's just that their brains thought they were. These kids were the best and fastest learners of all.

This led to the conclusion that **highly Stressed brains** are great at fast learning - primarily in relation to Survival needs. Instead, we want **calm, confident brains** that Thrive in learning new things.

Why do some smart kids switch off at school? In the mid 1990s, I became particularly interested in the correlation between dyspraxia, dyslexia, autism and attention deficit and hyperactivity. As a college tutor, I was especially keen to help stabilise the street kids who had already learned how to feel safer when running in packs. I could also see the mismatch of intellect and academic ability in our disaffected learners. They were often the smartest people.

In 1996, a school gate conversation led me to the pioneering work of the educational psychologist Madeleine Portwood. My friend was making a documentary about a neurological immaturity called dyspraxia (BBC2's *Heads, Shoulders, Knees and Toes*, aired January 1997) and through her I met and was privileged to learn from Madeleine.

The BBC documentary hypothesised that a high proportion of young offenders would profile as being very bright intellectually, but would have learning difficulties. In 'coping' or masking these problems, they would make poor choices around petty crime, drugs, alcohol, and risky behaviours. This was salient to me at the time and foundational for the future Happy Brain™ project.

In the documentary, Madeleine profiled young prisoners in HMP Deerbolt – a male Young Offenders' Institution in County Durham, England. The subsequent Deerbolt Study showed 61% of young offenders in the study profiled as dyspraxic.

Indeed, the backstories and narratives of the young offenders highlighted the stresses of 'coping' with their differences and how being in a 'gang' helped them to feel less 'stressed'.

In one of Madeleine's university lectures, I learned about the effects of a pressured and highly excitable limbic system. I also learned how to draw a neurological map and explain how the nervous system 'remembered things' - something that every class I now teach gets to see first-hand.

As I absorbed all the knowledge I could from this pioneer of neurodiversity, I still didn't know what to do with that information. **Now I do...**

Years later, I have written this book and amassed a massive body of information about how children grow their patterns of thought, feeling and behaviours from the early moments of life. I believe we must pay attention to these early patterns.

And where Happy Brain™ initially set out to help children and teachers boost creative learning (avoiding unruly, attention-seeking behaviours or social withdrawal) we now have a tried-and-tested model of skills for prevention *and* intervention.

I use a sausage machine analogy for my work. At one end of the machine, I deal with mental, emotional and behavioural 'outputs' that cause difficulties in adult life. There is an endless production of sausages with difficulties.

The other end of the sausage machine is where we can adjust the quality of ingredients entering the machine. However, the machinery itself only functions as well as the training skills, tools and attention of its maintenance crew.

Happy Brain™ training helps to build a machine that influences input, output and management/maintenance systems, starting with adults who can optimise the potential of our next generation. And in doing so, they cannot avoid optimising themselves.

iii. About this book

Through play and creativity, children are constantly showing and telling us how they are developing Thinking patterns and managing their feelings. Some of these patterns, if they are allowed to become habits, may not serve their future or adult selves well.

With mental health problems in our society at an all-time high, we must do something to change this trend now. So what can we learn from the children?

For more than a decade, I have gathered thousands of words, pictures and anecdotes from children of all ages that reveal *how* their young thoughts are already expanding or limiting their choices, very early in life.

I've used these examples to refine Happy Brain™ as a teaching model, inventing hundreds of games, activities and play materials that build resilience in children, families, classrooms and community groups. Now you can use some of them too.

Happy Brain™ is a tried-and-tested play-based teaching model that takes complex theories from science, education and psychology and transforms them into simple and accessible packets of knowledge and know-how to help children and teenagers thrive mentally, emotionally and physically.

In the following chapters you will discover how play and creativity affects the brain, boosting your confidence and directing your focus to know where, when and why to intervene, what to do next and which tools will best fast-track resilience.

Empirical evidence presented in this book comes from my professional career in teaching/coaching/therapy with children, teenagers and adults.

This book is for everyone, especially if you are a:
o   Parent, care provider, teacher
o   Social services professional
o   Mental or physical health professional
o   Interested in NLP, an NLP student, or a practitioner and/or trainer of NLP*

Happy Brain™ provides a sound introduction to Neuro Linguistic Programming (NLP) and offers a depth of understanding that took me years to figure, fast-tracking the ability to use NLP as a master structure and toolkit for Thrive. It is a tried-and-tested roadmap used globally, and my focus on using play and creativity to build resilience in children taps into the heart of NLP.

A note about consciousness

I often use a horse-riding analogy to help clients understand what I mean by brain training. Clearly, a horse is infinitely more powerful in strength and agility than any rider, yet an accomplished and congruent (thoughts, feelings and behaviours-aligned) rider will command compliance with precise responses. It's as if the two become a harmonious one.

Yet an inexperienced or incongruent (thoughts, feelings and behaviours out-of-alignment) rider will get either predictably limited responses or wildly variable results.

Mastering our minds is a bit like horse riding. The conscious (rider) part of our brain needs to be able to give and receive clean communication and give precise instructions to the unconscious (horse) part of our brain.

To become an accomplished rider, you need to develop coherent communication between yourself and your horse. To become an accomplished brain trainer, you need to develop coherent communication between the conscious and unconscious minds.

Throughout this book I'll use the terms 'conscious' and 'unconscious' as if they are two separate brain states, but of course that cannot be true; we experience ever-shifting states of consciousness, some more useful than others, as we shall see.

What is important here is that we form a common agreement of the terms used.

So, to be clear, Happy Brain™ refers to **different levels of conscious awareness:**
- o Of mind-body interactions
- o In abilities of self-determination
- o For oneself in relation to others

And now you know... so read on and enjoy!

CHAPTER ONE

"All models are wrong, but some are useful"

GEORGE BOX

STATISTICIAN (1919-2013)

CHAPTER ONE: HAPPY BRAIN™ IS A USEFUL MODEL

In this chapter, you will become familiar with Happy Brain™ as a useful model. This will help you to imagine the inner workings of the brain as a gateway to mental, emotional and physical wellbeing.

If it were possible to look inside your brain, you would discover a great deal of squishy, gooey white and grey matter filled with many secrets and mysteries that we humans are yet to unravel, though we do know there are trillions of pathways inside all that goo, continually firing electro-chemical messages.

Modern science generally acknowledges the human brain as evolving from the bottom-up, as follows:
- o **Old brain** – developing in utero shortly after conception
- o **Limbic system** – developing in toddlerhood
- o **Neo-cortex** – developing in early childhood and fully developed in early adulthood

Once these 3 brain parts have formed in sequence up from the base of the skull and merged, brain development moves forward into:
- o **Prefrontal cortex** – the new brain; the 'executive control centre'.

Ancient science provides a slightly different perspective, Plato documenting what he termed the 'triune soul', speculating that man was driven by 3 parts - gut, heart and head:
- o **Gut** - being the seat of basic desires and appetites
- o **Heart** - the seat of emotions and spiritedness
- o **Head** - (nous) the seat of conscious awareness and termed the rational mind

Mid-20th Century science brought us a brain model called Triune Brain theory:
- o **The Reptilian Brain** - orchestrating our instincts for survival
- o **The Mammalian Brain** - being our centre of emotions
- o **The Neo Cortex** - the seat of language, abstraction, planning, and perception

The Happy Brain™ Principles which follow are drawn from an amalgamation of the models listed above, combined with my own empirical experiences.

I'm a great believer in making everything in life as simple as possible, and this has been my mantra in building a model to help me to do my work.

During my teaching years, there was a lot of hype around the models of multiple intelligences and accelerated learning, and indeed these ideas opened our minds to consider the many ways in which children and adults assimilate information.

But I think these ideas fell short of their potential, thus failing many kids who would say: "I can't learn this because I'm only *visual*, only *musical*, only *mathematical...*' etc.

In creating the Happy Brain™ model, I was very mindful of these and many other learning models that I had embraced during my own studies.

I was particularly struck by Benjamin Bloom's Taxonomies of Learning, which explores three domains, as follows:

o Cognitive (mental) domain
o Affectual (emotional) domain
o Psychomotor (physical) domain

This resonates with the co-founder of Neuro Linguistic Programming (NLP), Dr Richard Bandler, when he says: "The quality of your thoughts affects the quality of your feelings, which in turn affects what you can and can't do."

I invite you to entertain the Happy Brain™ model in this book to find what inspires and engages you in helping children to think smarter, feel happier and behave with purpose. Beyond the model, you will find tried and tested activities, skills and tools.

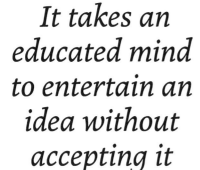

It takes an educated mind to entertain an idea without accepting it

ARISTOTLE

In the following chapters, you will explore and understand the 3 Principles of Happy Brain™:

i. Simplicity of understanding neuro-biological systems of learning
ii. Resilience found in self-managing emotions
iii. Clarity of making good decisions

o **Simplicity** of understanding neuro-biological systems of learning:
Neuro-biological systems of learning begin by being able to explain the neurophysiology of a Stressed child and of a calm child and knowing how to influence both systems through plain language and play.

o **Resilience** found in self-managing emotions:
Resilience comes from finding creative ways to experience, process and express a wide range of emotions. Our toolkit provides games to help children make better sense of their world.

o **Clarity** of making good decisions:
Clarity helps us to make good decisions and know what to do next.

Our activities help children to recognise and undo Thinking Traps. This happens in the prefrontal cortex, which we call the Thinking Mind.

3

INTRODUCING THE MODEL

I have designed a colourful model that is both memorable for adults and easy for kids to connect with.

The model is based on 3 brain 'parts' – the Reptilian Brain as a source of power for movement, the Mammalian Brain as the seat of emotions, and the prefrontal cortex as the Thinking Mind.

In the next four chapters, we are going to explore each of the 3 brain parts as if they were separate compartments, even though we know they are not, because the brain is one whole organism.

In doing this, we will learn to recognise which part we can learn to influence most easily to bring the whole brain back into Thrive.

4

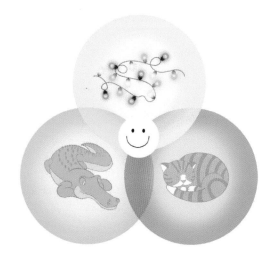

THRIVE BRAIN

This is where all three parts of the brain work in harmony together to support *eudemonia* – the term for human flourishing which was used by the Ancient Greeks.

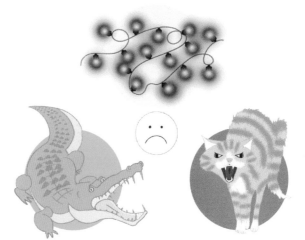

SURVIVE BRAIN
Where all three parts fragment and the brain's only goal is Survival by facing (assessing threat), fighting, fawning (super pleasing), flight (from threat), or freezing (feigning death).

STRESS BRAIN
Where there is disharmony that can mimic a Survival Brain or easily slide into that brain state, even without a threat being present. The key to resilience is recognising this brain state and taking steps to re-set it to Thrive.

CHAPTER TWO

*"Look to the nervous system as
the key to maximum health"*

GALEN OF PERGAMON

ANCIENT GREEK PHYSICIAN AND PHILOSOPHER

CHAPTER TWO: THE HAPPY BRAIN™ PRINCIPLE OF SIMPLICITY

In this chapter, we explore the brain's most primitive part, which we refer to as the Reptilian Brain.

SURVIVE

As outlined in the previous chapter, it helps if we sequence the brain from the 'bottom-up', and in our model, the Reptilian Brain is this primitive, lowest part, neurologically hard-wired to **Survive**. To do this, it needs to be able to react to danger by fighting or running away. Once safe, it can get on with the day-to-day business of resting, eating, exploring and finding ways to **Thrive**.

I encourage children to characterise this oldest brain 'part', which is primarily concerned with instinctive survival. Perhaps you can think of words to describe the crocodile characters of Survive, Stress, and Thrive on the right here, or think of names for them. It's useful to find a way to identify with these brain parts for future reference (note - *'part'* is my term, not an anatomically accurate description).

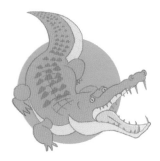

STRESS

Reptilian Brain functions are 'unconscious', which means they are automatic and continual, so they are active from just after conception through to death. Triggering the angry 'Survive' crocodile ignites an instant, hard-wired unconscious reaction. This instinctive reaction is not a conscious choice, but as you are about to discover, some aspects of Stress and Thrive can be influenced; this empowers us with choices about our responses and reactions to events.

The crocodile in our model is reacting to sensory information that is received and processed through the nervous system. Therefore, we need to understand a little more about this neurobiology...

THRIVE

8

Parents often ask me to *stop* their child's rage, tantrums, or other 'undesirable' behaviours, as if there were some magic button to press. Ironically, there is, only I would call it the nervous system.

Before we explore how to influence the nervous system, let's establish a simple understanding of it.

In the last chapter, I introduced the idea of the brain's electro-chemical signals firing trillions of messages between the brain and body. This primitive cluster of nerve signals makes up the brain and brain stem and is known as the **Central Nervous System (CNS).**

And from the CNS, the **Peripheral Nervous System** (PNS) branches out to all body parts, as you can see in the diagram, right.

*If you are aware of Neuro Linguistic Programming (NLP), you might want to think of this as the **Neuro** part of Neuro Linguistic Programming.*

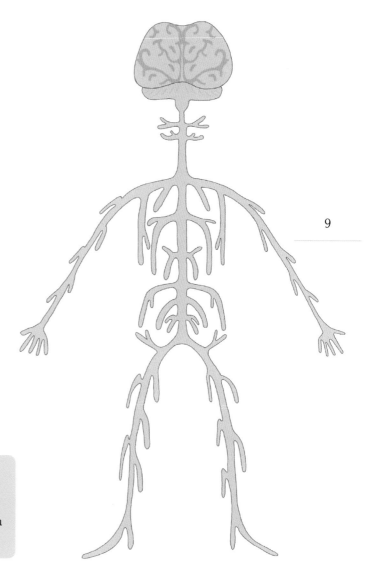

9

> **Next, we will explore the key functions of the Peripheral Nervous System (PNS) as follows:**
> o **Collecting/receiving sensory information**
> o **Processing/interpreting** this sensory information
> o **Reacting/responding** to the sensory information

Peripheral Nervous System Key Function 1
Collecting/receiving sensory information from the body and from the environment through sensory channels of sight (visual), sound (auditory), touch (tactile), smell (olfactory), taste (gustatory), enteric (gut), vestibular (balance), and proprioception (awareness of body positioning):

Peripheral Nervous System Key Function 2
Processing/interpreting this sensory information by sending signals through neurochemicals and brainwaves:

Neurochemicals: The human brain has around 100 neurotransmitters (chemical signals or messengers) whose actions help good-quality sensory processing.
The Happy Brain™ model focuses on 6 neurotransmitters that are key to what NLP calls 'good brain juice' and are easy to influence. We will explore these later.

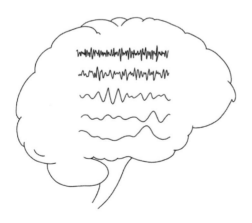

Brainwaves: The human brain also produces waveforms that are measured in hertz. Slow waves help the brain to rest and fast brainwaves help the brain to take action. We will also explore these later.

Peripheral Nervous System Key Function 3
Reacting/responding to sensory information:
A specific branch of the PNS, the Autonomic Nervous System (ANS) is key to the way we react/respond. It mobilises fats, sugars, electro-chemicals, hormones, and blood gasses which are all available to power an action. **This is your source of energy,** and it comes from two branches:

- o **Sympathetic** nervous system (SNS):
  Energy to **Survive** a threat/predator, by **facing** (to assess), **fighting** or **flighting** (run away).
  Energy to **Thrive** while supporting all daily activities.
  Energy of **Stress** for short bursts of extra *oomph*.
- o **Parasympathetic** nervous system (PSNS):
  Provides **rest energy** to **Thrive** through resting and digesting.

Occasionally, both systems - SNS & PSNS - 'jam'. When this happens, for example, if it is impossible to escape a threat, the system is immobilised to enable **Survival** by **freezing** (shutdown until safe to move) or **fawning** (super-pleasing).

11

THRIVE KEEPS THESE TWO
SYSTEMS (SNS & PSNS)
OPERATING IN HARMONY

Summary of the Peripheral Nervous System's key functions:
- o **Collecting/receiving sensory information.**
- o **Processing/interpreting** this sensory information.
- o **Reacting/responding** to the sensory information.

Later in this chapter, we will look at ways you can influence each of these functions.
First, let's turn our attention the simplicity of Survival.

SURVIVAL FIRST!

It's important to appreciate the value of a Survival reaction, e.g., stepping off the pavement without noticing an oncoming car and once startled by the sound of the car horn, all systems taking over to help you jump to safety. This is followed by the body trembling out any energy and very soon your breathing, pulse, etc. return to balance.

But if you start to recall the incident later and the thought alone triggers intense but unnecessary survival energy, what action is there to take? You cannot jump, scream, leap or run away while sitting in your armchair, so how can that stress energy be discharged?

Too many unmanaged thoughts, stresses and worries can simply trick the sympathetic energy system into **continually preparing the body to take action as a form of protection.**

This can result in something called 'sympathetic dominance' and this is a common feature in modern life. We want to (and can) change this through awareness and training, because if we don't, protection-oriented stress chemistry gets trapped, feels horrible and becomes toxic to wellbeing, as summarised below:

» Unmanaged Stress can trigger (unnecessary) survival reactions.

» Staying in a state of Stress prepares the nervous system to always be alert to danger and elevates the baseline for reactions.

» Staying in a state of Stress teaches the nervous system to make a habit of this.

» Habits build brain patterns that can become our default behaviours

» We rarely need a full 'Survival' reaction, and if we do, nature will help us re-set our energy systems. Re-setting your energy system is vital to wellbeing.

» If an analogy with nature helps, think about an electrical storm where pressure builds inside rain clouds. Sooner or later, the pent-up energy discharges (through lightning) into the ground. Then all is refreshed and rebalanced. Our survival reaction is like this; simple, swift and efficient. It is designed to re-set swiftly.

13

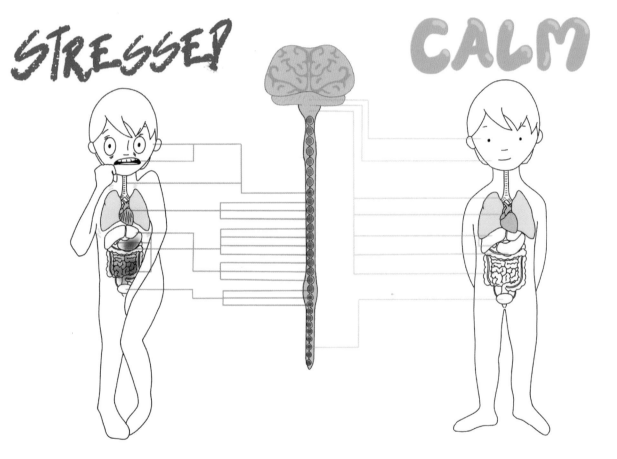

14

Identifying Stress

Many adults don't really understand how their body works. I think we have a responsibility to educate children about their biological systems and their influence on the way they feel and respond emotionally. I find diagrams like the one on the left make this simple. You can see how the sympathetic nervous system (the red lines) is bunched together for rapid communication with key body parts primed for survival. This illustration shows the physiological indicators of Stress detailed below.

These physiological indicators of Stress each have a purpose:

o *Fast, shallow* breathing quickly provides oxygen ready to fuel fight or flight reactions.
o *The digestive system* hurts from undigested food or fast elimination, as energies that were useful for digestion now divert to muscles needed for fight or flight. Digestive 'signals', e.g. for hunger, thirst, wee, poo, can be ignored.
o *Nail biting* is a self-soothing action that helps to release jaw tension.
o A folded-in or *rounded body* gives the illusion of being smaller and less visible to potential predators, while hunched shoulders keep the neck (spinal column) safe.
o *Clenched fists* 'hold in' and help to build up energy, just like the thunder cloud mentioned earlier.
o *Dilated pupils* maximise visual information and support hyper-vigilance.
o *Overeating* and fatigue helps a stressed body build and store energy reserves 'just in case' a sudden demand is required. Chewing also helps to release jaw tension.

The list goes on, and the reverse of these signs is generally true in Thrive, along with joy, spontaneity, singing, dancing, laughing.

This model is a guide for you to become aware of familiar Stress patterns. Consult a healthcare professional if your child exhibits any of these symptoms. We are not diagnosing Stress or ignoring underlying illnesses which may produce these symptoms.

15

> How might this model stimulate conversations with children about how their bodies work so they can 'take action' to de-stress rather than worry about 'what's wrong'?

SWITCHING ON YOUR THRIVE!

Training the nervous system to re-set quickly after Stress or to build the default patterns of Thrive is something we can all do.

Teaching children to be able to re-set their own Stress reaction and become less defensive builds confidence and self-esteem which in turn can positively influence behaviour.

To do this, we need to help young people to identity physiological sensations of Stress, be clear that the Stress is temporary, and then switch to a different neurological channel.

It's like watching bad TV - you have to do something to change the channel.

Activity:
BALLOON BREATHING

This is a simple technique that is proven to help people of all ages feel instantly calmer and more relaxed. It's easy to learn and can be practised anywhere.

Deep breathing into the lower lobes of the lungs, where the diaphragm pushes against part of the parasympathetic nervous system (the vagus nerve), tells the nervous system to switch off Stress and switch on calm. This remarkably simple yet powerful way to hack the nervous system into Thrive is written below as a script to be read to a child. That way the adult learns to do it too:

Imagine you have a balloon sitting right inside your tummy. Of course, you don't really have a balloon inside your tummy, but let's pretend you do because it will help you to feel calmer. What colour is your balloon? What kind of sound does your balloon make? I wonder what it would feel like if you could touch it.

As you take a big, deep breath in through your nose, you can imagine the air flowing deep down inside your tummy to fill the balloon. Now feel your tummy expanding with you in-breath until it is completely full and rounded.

Next, as you breathe out through your mouth you can imagine the balloon gently deflating and folding itself up.

Your balloon fills up even more as you make deeper in-breaths and your tummy will look like it has a balloon inside it when you make really deep in-breaths.

As you breathe out your tummy will feel like it's shrinking the balloon inside. Make your in-breath and out-breath last for the same amount of time – maybe each to a count of 3 or 4? Do this for about half a minute.

After a short while you can begin to make the out-

> ❝
> *Neurons that fire together, wire together*

DONALD HEBB
NEUROPSYCHOLOGIST

17

breath last longer than the in-breath – maybe in-breath for a count of 3 and out-breath for a count of 5 or 6? Do this for at least 1 minute.

Put your hand over your tummy to feel it get bigger and smaller as you breathe in and out for 1 minute. Inside your imagination, see, feel, hear and smell the balloon gently opening and closing as the out-breath lasts much longer than the in-breath. Where in your body do you feel most relaxed? Perhaps it's your shoulders, or your back? Maybe it's somewhere else?

Where will you practise this next?
At school? Before bed? Before homework?
After breaktime excitement?
Somewhere else?"

Repeat this daily for 21 days to make sure your nervous system knows how to do it automatically.

Your nervous system is like a map

Every second of every moment, your nervous system is being bombarded by billions of fragments of sensory information. The nervous system receives, processes and reacts to this information by building a neurological 'map' of its existence.

Neural pathways connect neurons (nerve cells) that transmit messages. We don't grow neurons (baby brains have the same number of them as adult brains) but we do grow and prune the connections between them, which we call neural pathways.

Neural pathways are formed, strengthened or diminished according to:
o **Frequency** of use
o **Quality** and **combination** of neurochemicals and neuroreceptors
o **Intensity** and **coherence** of brainwaves

To help you to visualise this, imagine a new-born baby's brain with instinctive/hereditary pathways and a lifetime of neurological potential. Over time and depending on life experiences, the neurological map evolves to make certain things more important than others.

Kids love imagining, drawing and chatting about their 'evolving' maps, and I often use toy cars to create movement (forward, reverse, stop, go etc) and explore interaction with other vehicles. We might add stop/go flags and note which signposts are built by other people or by oneself. We can be super-creative playing in the map of daily adventures, and get curious about the adventures which lie beyond the current 'map'. Sometimes, there are other cars which cause diversions and crashes, and maybe a road sweeper or rescue vehicle pops up on the road.

Once this metaphor is established, I can help clients to learn something fundamental to their future

happiness, e.g. while some pathways/roads may be hard-wired (non-negotiable) neurological patterns of survival reactions, most others are simply the result of use.

Therefore, neural pathways:
o Have to be created
o Have to be repeatedly driven to make them stronger
o Have to be rewarding in some way in order to keep them in use
o Can mostly be overwritten using a bit of Tipex (the original line still exists, but a newer version is easy to access)

There is a saying that goes something like 'if you always do what you always did, you always get the same results' which can be demonstrated perfectly in our metaphor.

QUICK SUMMARY

Your neurological map is made up of:
o **Codes** - combinations of sensory information, neurochemicals, and brainwaves
o **Patterns** of habitual used neural pathways that act as your auto-routes
o Hard-wired pathways that **prioritise** survival programmes
o Thrive patterns that **strengthen** if used regularly and **fade** if hardly/never used
o Codes and patterns that can and do change through **neuroplasticity** (the brain's ability to continually change)

Case Study: Adam's colour-coded behaviour

Seven-year-old Adam came to me to learn how to deal with his feelings of rage. According to his mum, his tantrums regularly lasted 45 minutes when he became stuck in an un-resourceful state.

You will remember from earlier in this chapter, with the illustration of the reaction to a beeping car horn, that an ongoing 'rage' (beyond an acute threat) is the result of un-managed stress. Adam needed new ways to take charge of his behaviour when he became 'stuck' like this.

I asked Adam to make an illustration of his brain exploring a traffic light analogy. He decided the colour red would represent his angry brain pathways and codes, green would be the colour of his Happy Brain™ pathways and codes, and orange would be the colour of his helper brain pathways and codes that helped him to re-direct his behaviours.

Next, we got busy chatting about having fun and feeling really proud of his behaviours, and Adam drew these happy/proud codes and pathways (fig 1):

This picture now carried 'meaning' to Adam's unconscious mind because his neurology now associated the sensory experience of the drawing with brainwaves and the chemistry of feeling happy.

We had 'anchored' – fixed - his attention into this sensory code, which would now be available to me to use as a resource should I want to re-trigger these happy feelings. In NLP, this process of associating a sensory code to particular feeling is called 'anchoring'.

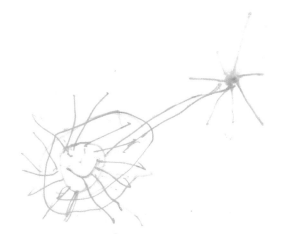

19

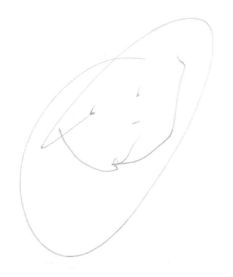

(fig 1)

20

(fig 2)

Next, we chatted about things and situations that made Adam feel angry, sad or mad. I encouraged him to feel those feelings in his body before he drew on his map (fig 2).

Until now, Adam's brain had been used to getting stuck in the red paths and codes, sometimes for up to 45 minutes, and so, having associated Adam's feelings of anger to the drawing, I needed to break him away from these feelings.

So, to interrupt the 'pattern' we played with my dogs. This is an example of a 'pattern interrupt' - another NLP technique. It works when a brain pattern that is used to habitually firing in a particular sequence is unexpectedly re-directed, forcing the pattern to behave differently.

However, without a significant emotion to glue the new pattern (next chapter), or repetition of use to strengthen it, the new pathway can easily become overwritten; for Adam, there was still more work to do.

(fig 3)

Adam giggled when we acted out handing over his red brain thoughts to my dog Oscar. Laughter changes brain chemistry, so the chemistry of laughter gently softened the strength of red neural connections. At the same time I was tempting Adam's neurological map to grow new routes to take when dealing with anger, as he could now imagine handing over red brain 'thoughts' to Oscar the dog.

However, we still needed an additional tool to help him to re-direct the old pathways of rage, so we plotted some 'little brain helper buddies' - the orange team, explorers of smart ideas and possibilities.

In Adam's imagination, as these little orange guys went about their work, they made sounds like fingers working on a computer keyboard (fig 3).

Now we had three colour-coded behaviours - resources for Adam and me to play with inside his brain (neurological) map and discover more routes to help him to help himself moving forward.

I photocopied each drawing, Adam cut them out and then we laminated them (I made the red parts smallest and green parts biggest as unconscious indicators of power) so we could play the games over the page.

ADAM'S GAMES

1. **Flash card charades**

   Acting out the 3 major feelings and their different sensations in sequence – red, orange, green – teaches the neurology to keep processing until the good (green) brain neural pathway. Previously, Adam had become stuck in red. Now his brain knew how to move on to green (with his little brain buddies' help). NLP calls this technique 'chaining anchors'.

2. **Splat!**

   While accessing the red brain problem, Adam could take the green brain and physically SPLAT in on top of the red one, making an exaggerated 'Splat!' noise. This metaphor uses sound, sight and action to generate a sense of control. It forges new neural pathways.

3. **Squish**

   If 'Splat!' wasn't enough, Adam would take the orange brain and Squish (a side-to-side movement) the red. Next, I taught him to take 3 balloon breaths and blow each out onto the orange brain. On the last out-breath, he gently placed the green brain on top. Balloon Breathing switches off a stress reaction inside the nervous system, so doing this really stacks the chances of success, putting Adam in control of his Thrive Drive.

4. **Visualisation**

   Closed eye '*imagineering*' of each of these activities firmly imprints the processes onto the mind's eye, building strong neural networks for different behavioural responses. In doing this, Adam was mentally rehearsing his future success.

Visualisation: The brain doesn't know the difference between externally real sensory experience and imagined sensory experience, so it explores **both** inside the map. This is the power of mental rehearsal!

Teaching Adam to change his reactions helped him to discover behavioural flexibility - a gift for life. He also unglued his identity as a 'naughty boy' as he realised his behaviour had simply become stuck in inappropriate reactions to certain stimuli. He was now free to better manage his feelings and therefore make better decisions. Adam's mum wrote to me a few weeks later, delighted to report no further tantrums. That was 45 minutes of tantrums to nil in just a few weeks of practising new ways to run his brain. Today, 12 years later, Adam is a calm, confident and delightful 19-year-old. Things could have turned out very differently had he remained unable to change the connections inside his brain that then helped him self-manage his rage. Thankfully, his parents understood the importance of these 'play techniques'.

Perhaps the next time you are stuck at a red traffic light, you can remind yourself about deep balloon breaths that activate orange brain buddies to **keep the flow until it's green to go...**

22

INFLUENCING SENSORY INFORMATION

Let's look at how we can influence the quality of the bonds that determine how we respond to the world in which we live. These become our autopilot!

We make sense of our world throughout life by receiving, processing and responding to sensory stimuli. Ideally, we are able to find a workable balance between **incoming sensory information** (from the outside world) and **outgoing sensory information** (from the inside world).

Sometimes we get out of **balance** and rely too much on either the inside or outside.

Brain training is a lot to do with helping people to **re-balance**.

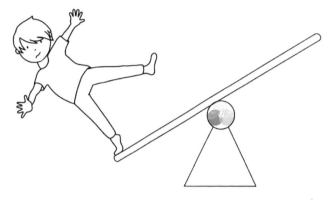

23

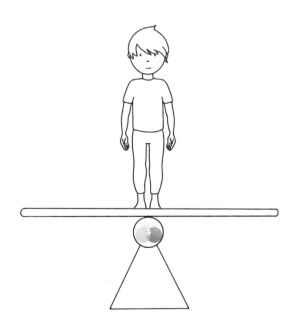

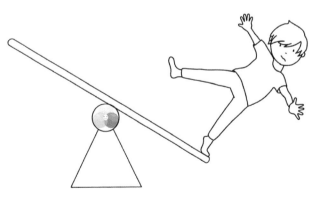

Since Happy Brain™ is about the prevention of these neurological biases, we look at ways to help set up the best possible quality of information to be received and processed. The first step to take is becoming consciously aware of your sensory channels and then exercising them. **Mindfulness** is a great way to begin doing this.

24

In my workshops and coaching sessions with children, we play many **sensory tune-up games** such as Eye-Spy, Ear-Hears, Feel-Feels, Nose-Knows, Tongue-Tastes, each drawing attention to specific bits of sensory information.

A favourite activity I use with kids is based on a laminated print-out of sensory images with a 'spinning arrowhead' placed in the middle of the picture.

I then ask the children questions about each of the senses, for example:

Remembered information from the past that is subjective, internally referenced from previous encoding in neurological map, eg. '*I can remember the sound of my doorbell ringing*'.

Present information that can be verified by someone present, eg. '*I can see the sun shining*'.

Imagined information about the future that is subjective, internally referencing previous encoding in neurological map and creating new patterns, eg. '*I can imagine the texture of the cake I will make on Monday*'.

Making these subtle sensory distinctions will have a profound effect on the way children are able to de-construct future problems, as we shall see in later chapters. Many emotions run high when there is confusion about sensory information that the brain thinks is real (in the present moment) when in fact it is imagined or remembered. This game exercises the sensory channels.

The next exercise is a **Sensory Mind Spa,** which is a bit like a brain gym for sensory channels.

You need to set aside some time to do this, but it really helps the nervous system to collect and process 'precise' sensory data, which is another skill for resilience.

I'll expand on the benefits of these foundational activities in later chapters, when you will discover how strategies for Thrive depend on collecting and processing the best-quality sensory information.

Activity: The Sensory Mind Spa

Ideally, practise this exercise in nature...

i. VISUAL

Far – Near: Look for the farthest object you can see. Stay focused on it for several moments. No need to name it or chat about it, just observe. After a few minutes, bring your full attention to a close-up object, allowing your vision to adjust and tune in. Repeat.

General – Specific: Slightly defocus your eyes and expand your peripheral vision so that you get a full overview of the whole picture, including the outer limits of your vision and general movement. Notice how this technique automatically relaxes you. Then bring your focus onto something very specific and tune in to a still detail. Repeat.

Flat – 3D: Find a bush or tree and look at it as though you were about to paint it on a flat, 1D surface. Now look through it and create a 3D effect inside your mind's eye. Repeat.

Mind photography – testing the neural pathways: Gaze at a specific detail, e.g. a flower head. No analysis. Take a photo of it in your mind's eye. Now close your eyes and recall the picture as a digital image, then repeat and recall it as a movie. Repeat.

Feel the effects of your visual mini mind spa!

ii. HEARING

Far – Near: Listen for the farthest sound you can hear. Stay focused on it for several moments. No need to name it or chat about it, just listen. After a few minutes bring your full attention to a close-up sound, allowing your hearing to adjust and tune in. Repeat.

General – Specific: Hear the whole symphony of your environment by expanding your peripheral hearing to get a sense of the general sounds. Notice how this technique automatically relaxes you. Then listen to a very specific sound by tuning in to a precise detail. Repeat.

Rhythmic – Singular: Listen for a rhythm of nature, a sound or beat that repeats. Trace the rhythm by excluding other sounds. Now trace random sounds coming from different directions. Repeat.

Aural photography – testing the neural pathways: Listen to one sound of nature. No analysis. Record a soundbite of it in your mind's ear. Now recall the sound as if it were a digital recording. Repeat.

Feel the effects of your hearing mini mind spa. Did you find it easier to tune into this auditory channel by closing your eyes?

A note about hearing: The auditory sense is the first to develop in utero. It is designed to receive, process and react to soundwaves 24/7, for life, unlike other sensory channels that may 'rest'. Our survival reactions and thrive responses can be stimulated by soundwaves alone through voice (our own or others) or other sounds, including music. This helps to explain why music, singing, talking, chanting, humming, etc. can influence us.

iii. TASTE
Take a plate of everyday food, close your eyes and taste the subtle differences: Bitter–Sweet–Sour | High-Low-Medium tones | Warming–Cooling | Astringent–Hydrating | After-taste

Testing the neural pathways: Let go of the physical experience and tune in to your memory. Recall the taste of each item of food. No analysis, just imagination.

Feel the effects of your gustatory mini mind spa. Did you find it easier to tune in to this channel by closing your eyes?

iv. DIGESTION
Eat only one type of food or drink only one kind of drink at a time, the notice the following:

Mouth: What happens to the food in your mouth as saliva helps begin the digestion process? Notice how quickly or slowly you roll, chew and swallow your food. How do you know when to start/stop eating?

Stomach: How does the food/drink feel in the stomach; light, heavy, still, moving? What are the sensation 'signals' of hunger and thirst?

Intestine/colon: Does your gut feel spacious or constricted? Can you perceive the difference between left and right side?

Pee and poo: Which foods help or hinder 'elimination'? What sensations signal needing to pee or poo? As a mind experiment, try Balloon Breathing before using the toilet and notice the effect relaxation has on elimination.

Testing the neural pathways: Let go of the physical experience and tune in to your memory. One by one, recall the feel of each experience. No analysis, just imagination.

Feel the effects of your digestion mini mind spa. Did you find it easier to tune in to this channel by closing your eyes?

v. TOUCH
Touch and feel several things/objects and gently experience the skin's perception. Close your eyes and feel the many subtle differences:

Texture: Contrast rough with smooth.
Temperature: Contrast warmth and cold.
Moisture: Contrast dampness and dryness.

Testing the neural pathways: Let go of the physical experience and tune in to your memory. One by one, recall the feel of each experience. No analysis here, just imagination.

Feel the effects of your tactile mini mind spa. Did you find it easier to tune in to this channel by closing your eyes?

vi. BALANCE

Find several surfaces and gently experience your sense of balance. If you can, close your eyes and feel the many subtle differences in your internal perception. Then repeat in front of a mirror to check your external perception of balance.

Symmetrically balanced: Stand or sit still, feel the internal/external balance.
Off balance: Stand or sit in a deliberately awkward position.
Re-balanced: Stand on one leg and wait until you adjust to find balance.
Testing the neural pathways: Let go of the physical experience and tune in to your memory. One by one recall the feel of each experience. No analysis, just imagination.

Feel the effects of your balance mini mind spa.
What was the difference between eyes open (external feedback) and eyes closed -(internal feedback)?

vii. BODY AWARENESS

Walk, run, cycle, swim and notice the many subtle differences in your internal perception. Experiment with forward, backward and sideways movements.

Symmetrically balanced: How balanced and symmetrical does your body feel?
Mechanics of movement: How does your body organise its joints, muscles, tendons, ligaments, etc to create movement?
Flow: Are you in a smooth or jerky interaction with the air/water?
Testing the neural pathways: Let go of the physical experience and tune in to your memory. One by one recall the feel of each experience. No analysis, just imagination.

Feel the effects of your body awareness mini mind spa. What was the difference between the forward, backward, sideways movements?

viii. SMELL

Fill a plate with food or other things such as flowers, toiletries, clothing, etc. and gently experience the distinctions of your olfactory nerve. This is the only sense that feeds directly into the primitive brain and is therefore key to our evolution. Keep it in good order!

Close your eyes and smell the many subtle differences:
Fragrances: Bitter – Sweet | High – Low tones | Warming – Cooling
Perception: Attracting – Repelling | Fresh – Stale | Moving – Still
Testing the neural pathways: Let go of the physical experience and tune in to your memory. One by one recall the smell of each experience. No analysis, just imagination.

A note on smell: The olfactory bulb is the only sensory input directly linked into the brain's 'smoke alarm' for Threat; the amygdala. This suggests the importance of smell in our processing of perceived threat.

27

Neurochemicals

There are said to be around 100 neurochemicals vital to our wellbeing, both for Survival and for Thrive, all ebbing and flowing in a multitude of combinations.

The 3 major stress chemicals are adrenaline, cortisol, and norepinephrine and they help to power fight or flight reactions, which is important in appropriate situations, but we don't want them to dominate the quality of our brain chemistry.

My super 6 neurochemicals (below) are no more important than the other 94, but they are listed here because they are easy for you to research and easy for us all to influence:

- o **Serotonin** Often referred to as the 'happiness molecule'. Essential for self-esteem and feeling calm. Promote through relaxation, deep breathing e.g. Balloon Breathing, meditation, bath soaks, and diet (e.g. good quality 85% cacao chocolate and herbs such as St. John's Wort**)

- o **Oxytocin** Known as the *hug hormone*, this is essential for social bonding. Mothers and newborn babies are flooded with oxytocin (nature is very smart). Promote through skin touch e.g. hand holding, hugs, massage, cooperative activities, and herbs such as chamomile* and lavender*.

- o **Endorphin** Nature's 'high' that provides an analgesic effect. Promote through walking, dancing, exercise and laughter.

- o **GABA** This is known as *nature's valium* since it regulates anxiety by blocking or inhibiting stress chemicals. It also helps to support bodily movement. Promote through whole foods and vegetables, fermented foods, and herbs such as chamomile* and lavender*.

- o **Dopamine** The feel-good reward for taking action sets up motivation circuits. Promote through novelty, music, sport, dairy, omega 3, nuts and protein rich foods.

- o **Acetylcholine** Helps to support memory signals, especially through deep restorative sleep. Supports movements. Promote through choline foods (eggs, fish, meats and whole grains) and herbs such as sage* and rosemary*.

*I use herbal teas and essential oils to help prepare myself – or my environment - for the task ahead.
I may want to calm my nervous system (lavender or chamomile), liven it up (bergamot or lime), or help memory (rosemary or sage).
Note - *This is not prescriptive; you should always consult a health professional or medical herbalist before making dietary changes. **St John's Wort is known to interact with medication – please seek advice before using.*

I've referenced a few simple herbs on the page opposite because they have great impact on brain function. For example:

o Phytochemicals in **lavender** inhibit sympathetic nervous system & bind with GABA receptors.

o Phytochemicals in **chamomile** bind with GABA receptors.

If you want to find out more about the effect of herbs on brain chemistry, check out Dilston Physic Garden in Northumberland. I'm a student and trustee of this amazing place and have been hugely influenced by the work of neuroscientists Professor Elaine Perry and Nic Perry PhD. www.dilstonphysicgarden.com

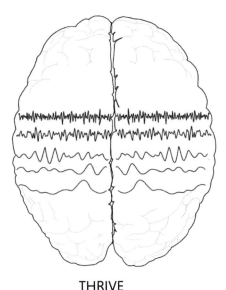
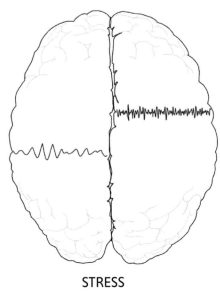

THRIVE
(coherent) brainwaves

STRESS
(incoherent) brainwaves

BRAINWAVES

Think of the seashore and you will likely recall the sound of waves as they connect with the shoreline. Waves of energy may caress the shore, or violently crash upon it. You can visualise a wave and the variable waveforms.

The human brain also produces waveforms (electrochemical) that can be measured as dynamic patterns throughout the whole brain.

They continually change in reaction or response to the nervous system's reactions to the world. For example, the sound of someone screaming would immediately produce fast waves to support fight/flight energy needs.

Actually, what is key here is not necessarily the strength ('amplitude') or the frequency of brainwaves, but how the right and left hemispheres synchronise the wave forms.

o **Thrive** brainwaves do this, and we call it 'coherence'.

o **Stress** brainwaves are not coherent and prompt our natural bias to one hemisphere, for example to blame others (*left hemisphere bias*) or to blame self (*right hemisphere bias*). When the two hemispheres are out of sync, it contributes to dissonance within the mind and body.

In our model, we generalise the notion that the right hemisphere is the seat of creativity and intuition, while the left hemisphere is more logical and rational. The diagram above illustrates the contrast in coherent (Thrive) and incoherent (Stress) brainwaves.

Brainwaves are measured in hertz (cycles per second). 1 hertz (hz) is an equivalent frequency to 1 heartbeat, so 1 heartbeat per second is the same frequency as 1 hz. Here is a brief overview of brainwaves:

o **Delta: 0.1-3 hz** Very slow wave forms found in sleep and very deep meditation. At this frequency, the brain can do its pruning (clean-up) of neural pathways that are no longer priority connections.

o **Theta: 3-8 hz** Slow brainwaves of a semi-conscious and highly suggestible brain that fast tracks **re-programming and super-learning.** Theta brainwaves are dominant in children under 7, who experience the most accelerated learning of all. Theta can be accessed through **visualisation and meditation.**

o **Alpha: 7-12 hz** Quite slow brainwaves which enable **relaxation and generative learning.**

o **Beta: 12-30 hz** Fast brainwaves which are a baseline for everyday **complex thinking.** High Beta is linked to 'over-thinking'.

o **Gamma: > 30 hz** Very fast brainwaves which enable **peak performance.** Gamma is also found in hyper-vigilance (alert to danger) and fragmented but fast learning.

Neuro-feedback equipment is easy to access and fun to use if you want to see your brainwaves in real time.

Balloon Breathing helps to slow down brainwaves and build coherence between the two hemispheres, as does listening to classical music, because the brain naturally tries to synchronise to the external waveform. You may have heard of *mirror neurons* or *brain entrainment*. Our brains naturally seek to resonate at the same wavelength as the primary social group (more on that later) which helps to explain how you can 'pick up' someone else's stress.

Sounds have an instant effect on brainwaves (either calming or alerting); one of the most powerful ways you can influence someone else's brainwaves is by speaking in a calm, gentle, low tone. It doesn't matter what you are saying - this primitive part of your brain is searching for clues about its safety. When you start listening to the 'music' behind someone's voice you can pick up clues about their brainwaves.

This is especially true for children, because from birth to around age 7 a child's neurology is hard-wired to imprint from its primary caregiver(s), and this includes synchronising brainwaves with them, which makes good Survival sense when you think about it.

Perhaps you can think about times when a young child 'picked up' your Stress?

It is imperative that a child is dependent on external signals of danger. It's a marvellous survival mechanism developed long before language centres are formed. If you are a parent or work with children, I invite you to think a bit about how you manage your own stress long before you seek help for a stressed child who may be simply mimicking your brain patterns. Take the example of Jack and his mum Marie: Jack was 4 years old when Marie asked me to stop his angry outbursts that in turn **made her very angry.** She wanted him to change his behaviour *so she didn't have to feel so stressed* in social situations, where she obsessed that Jack 'might' misbehave.

The simplest solution was to teach mum how to train her own calm, confident states, but it was hard to convince her that her own stress patterns were a large part of the problem. Instead, she believed her child had a problem and needed help.

In NLP, we talk about 'state' and how to *go there first*, i.e. get yourself into the energy state you want someone else to follow. **The strongest, most congruent and coherent brainwaves will have the biggest influence.**

31

Activity: Finding feelings

The autonomic nervous system - the control system which acts largely unconsciously introduced earlier in this chapter - tells your body what actions to take. Sometimes, these actions are subliminal, for example, a twitch of a finger or a micro-movement in the face. Sometimes, these actions are more noticeable, e.g. leaning forwards or backwards while chatting (as if trying to get closer to the subject or move farther away).

Becoming aware that these physiological sensations are simply electro-chemical messages can have an extremely positive effect on resilience.

Children are remarkably accurate in perceiving their peers' energy and can draw/paint interpretations of waveforms that look very similar to the readings of bio- or neuro-feedback machines. Encouraging children to identify their physical sensations by pointing to and describing their somatic (bodily) sensations is fun and usually quite simple. It is adults who often 'don't get' that they can tune into and express the nervous system's sensations (e.g. *'my skin tingles'* or *'my stomach feels solid'*), without adding labels or judgements, such as the feeling is 'anxiety', or labelling it 'a bad feeling'.

This activity is fun to do in a group, or can be done on your own or 1:1 with a child.

Draw three bodily outlines labelled:
o **Thrive** sensations
o **Survive** sensations
o **Stress** sensations

Think about the creative ways we might express the 'subtle' energy systems that the Reptilian Brain is busy regulating. Draw, paint, use glitter (or whatever creative means you choose) to express the physiological sensations of states such as accelerated heart rate, tingly tummy, dry mouth, sweating etc.

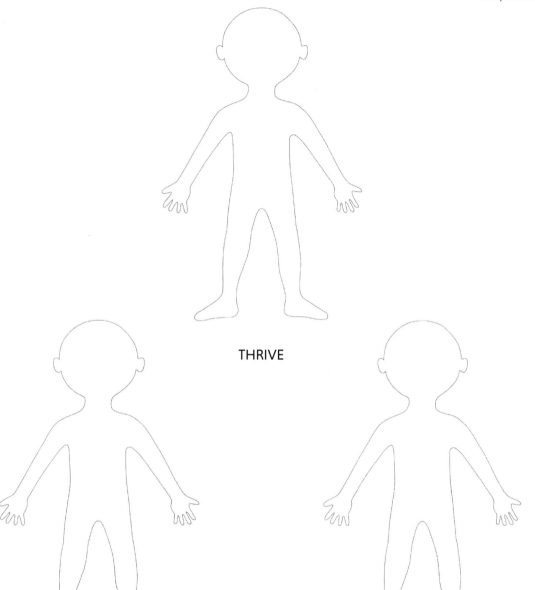

THRIVE

SURVIVE

STRESS

Now repeat the same exercise using only words. Find descriptions of the sensations. Here are some words that may help:

ACHY	AIRY	BLOATED	BLOCKING
BLOCKED	BOILING	BREATHLESS	BUBBLY
BURSTING	BUTTERFLIES	BUZZY	CALM
CLENCHED	CLOSED	COLD	COMFORTABLE
CONGESTED	CONSTRICTED	CONTRACTED	COOL
DARK	DEHYDRATED	DISCONNECTED	DIZZY
DRAINED	DRY-MOUTHED	DULL	EMPTY
FULL	ENERGETIC	ENERGISED	EXHAUSTED
EXPANDED	EXPANSIVE	FAINT	FLEXIBLE
FLOATING	FLOATY	FLOPPY	FLUID
FLUTTERY	FROZEN	GIDDY	GROUNDED
HEADACHEY	HEAVY	HOLLOW	HOT
HUNGRY	HURTING	ICY	ITCHY
JABBING	JITTERY	JUMPY	KNOTTED
LIGHT	LIGHT-HEADED	LIMP	NAUSEOUS
NERVY	NERVOUS	NUMB	OPEN
PARCHED	POUNDING	PRESSURE	PRICKLY
PULSING	QUEASY	QUIVERING	RADIATING
RAVENOUS	RAW	RELAXED	RELEASED

RIGID	SAGGY	SATIATED	SATISFIED
SENSITIVE	SHAKY	SHIVERY	SHORT
SHORT OF BREATH	SHUDDERING	SICK	SPACEY
SPACIOUS	SPONGY	SQUASHED	SQUASHY
SQUIRMY	STABBING	STINGING	STRETCHY
STUFFED	SUFFOCATED	SWEATY	TALL
TAUT	TEARFUL	TEARY	TENSE
THICK HEADED	THROBBING	TICKLY	TIGHT
TINGLING	TINGLY	TIRED	TREMBLY
TWITCHY	TREMBLING	UNCOMFORTABLE	VIBRATING
FIZZY	WARM	WOBBLY	WET
WOOZY	DRAINING	LIFTING	DETACHED
OUTSIDE BODY			

Taking away the interpretation of physical experience as '*meaning something*' helps you to connect to the part of the brain that is producing the physical sensation, keeping the story-telling mind out of the equation.

We'll look at this in much more detail later.

36

STRESS TRAP

Stress so often gets trapped in the nervous system because we try to get away from it by focusing too much on it or labelling it. For example, saying "I feel anxious" does not tell your nervous system what to do next.

Next time this happens, try describing the sensation (as above) and then thinking about a new way of sequencing the sensory information, either in the **direction** of movement, or the **intensity** of the sensation. Most people can make a feeling more intense, which is good, because if you can move it at all, you can move it on purpose. Now to convince people this a rewarding thing to do…

Giving Stress sensations somewhere to move is a gift you can offer other people, especially children who haven't yet become bound to any perceived benefits of holding on to Stress. You could say something like:

- o "So that wobbly feeling in your leg, how can you let it keep wobbling down through the soles of your feet and into the ground?"
- o "So that feeling of pressure in your head, where in your body can you find the opposite of that feeling? And where in your body can you let the two sensations meet?"

Coaching tip

In this example, notice the effect that language has on the other person's neurology:

"So that wobbly feeling in your leg…"

With these words, you are simply pacing the reality of the other person's experience by reflecting back the exact words you have heard them say.

This helps their brain to feel reassured that you understand them. It may even stop them holding onto the feeling while trying to convince you that something is wrong.

"How can you let it keep wobbling down through the soles of your feet and into the ground?"

Asking 'how' invites the other person to explore the possibility that they could do this, thus forging new neurological pathways of imagination that will help them later.

Activity: Spinning feelings

Building on Finding Feelings above, this technique comes from the work of Dr. Richard Bandler (www.purenlp.com) who noticed that when a client described their problem (or solution) they would involuntarily use gestures to indicate what was happening inside their nervous system, often with a hand motion. He experimented with having the client pay attention to the sensations (as in the last exercise) and then consciously altering the flow. Almost every time, the client could make themselves feel better or worse – on purpose.

Once you have become familiar with the sensations of Survive/Thrive, you can notice how specific feelings move, in particular around the solar plexus (in the pit of the stomach) where there is a particularly rich concentration of nerve fibres (the vagus nerve mentioned earlier).

Common sensations have a movement rotating clockwise, anti-clockwise, tumbling forward or tumbling backwards.

Once your child has found the movement, ask them to create a 'circuit' from where it starts to where it ends, looping it back on itself. Now have them spin the movement faster, slower and in different directions to discover what makes the sensation increase or decrease, i.e. better or worse. This is a super-fast way to feel in control of your nervous system response. Many teenagers value this technique before an exam or if they're feeling nervous about a social event. It works – try it yourself. It will work even faster when we engage other brain parts in later chapters.

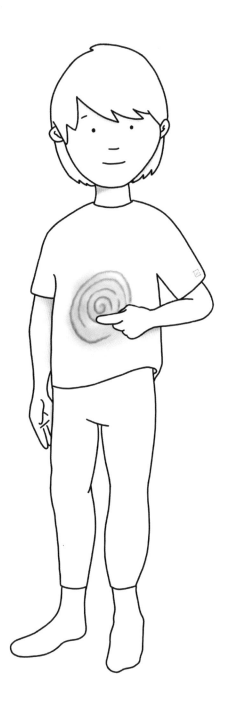

Activity: Playing inside your neurological map

Think of a great memory; one where you felt really, really happy.

Now use your mind's eye and ear to 'step into' the memory, as if you are there again, looking through your own eyes and hearing all the sounds around you. Point to the happy feeling inside your body. Now speed up the sensations and then slow them down. Change the direction of the feelings and keep experimenting until you can increase and spread the sensation of happiness just by thinking about it.

Congratulations! In doing this, you have just taken the reins of your own autonomic nervous system and taught it to do something specific, on purpose. This is what we call brain training...

What if?

What if you were to play inside your neurological map like this every day? What could the benefits be to your health if you used your memory senses to saturate your neurology in great brain juice and coherent brainwaves?

Is it possible that until now, you've practised saturating your neurology in stress brain juice and incoherent brainwaves? People do say, '*whatever you practise, you get good at...*'

Now teach a child to do this and build happiness as a default neurological pattern.

Summary: The Principle of Simplicity

In this chapter we have explored the Reptilian Brain's need for survival and protection, and established that the need to feel protected, safe and secure trumps everything.

We've looked at the role of the peripheral nervous system in receiving, processing and reacting to sensory data, and how we can influence the quality of sensory data. We've explored brain chemistry and brainwaves to illustrate our model as a useful way to help people Thrive. In particular, we're interested in influencing the

autonomic nervous system to switch off stress and habituate thrive states.

This is a generative learning model with many layers to unfold in the coming chapters. In the next chapter, we will connect this chapter's Reptilian Brain to its co-creator of happiness, the Mammalian Brain.

BEFORE WE MOVE ON, PLEASE CAPTURE YOUR THOUGHTS:

» Questions

» Comments

» Insights

CHAPTER THREE

"I don't want to be at the mercy of my emotions. I want to use them, enjoy them, and dominate them"

OSCAR WILDE

POET AND PLAYWRIGHT (1854-1900)

CHAPTER THREE: THE PRINCIPLE OF RESILIENCE

In the last chapter, we explored the role of the Reptilian Brain in preparing the body to take action. In this chapter, we will look at the Mammalian Brain's role in regulating communication between the Reptilian Brain (lower region) and the Thinking Mind (higher region) as well as communicating with the outside world.

SURVIVE   STRESS   THRIVE

In this Happy Brain™ principle, we propose that the Mammalian Brain is hard-wired to make certain things **feel important** in order that they can stay *really memorable* for future reference and help us to make decisions.

To do this, chemical markers known as **emotions** anchor (or glue) strong feelings to specific behaviours in the evolving neurological map. This is the 'middle' part of our model and has the very important task of communicating between the bottom (Reptilian) and top (Thinking) brain parts. **This middle brain part is key to developing resilience.** We are going to look at how the Mammalian Brain helps us to give/

receive **attention** to/from other humans. This may be the trickiest part of the brain to 'train' - hence the cat illustration - but the rewards are plentiful.

In our model, we view emotions as chemical signals that help to:
- o *Give and receive **attention** from the outside world*
- o *Make strong feelings super **valuable***
- o *Make important patterns more **accessible***
- o *Add meaning to the sensory information to make it more **memorable***

We know from the last chapter that repeating behaviours makes stronger neural pathways and thus learning can happen through **frequency** of doing.

Now we look at adding *intensity* of feelings to help glue specific memories into the brain's neurological map, thus learning can happen through **intensity** of feeling.

Much of this chapter is written through the lens of a child's emotional development because this is a very child-like part of our behaviour.

ATTENTION

It seems that there is a universal language amongst animal babies; expressing their *survival* needs from birth. In human babies, long before using language, a child needs to **communicate** to primary caregivers the need for nutrition, hydration, comfort, shelter, warmth and safety, and a child quickly learns their caregivers' variable responses to differing cries. Thus, a non-verbal language emerges.

From the very beginning, a child's neurology is recording reactions and responses to sensory experiences. This is why you may have noticed children responding differently to different people in different situations.

As *social animals,* we value attention, guidance and wisdom from our 'tribe' members (family, friends, social groups) and quickly learn patterns of communication that not only get us attention, they also teach us how to influence others to behave differently.

Habits form fast, as we saw in the last chapter. For

example, a child who learns that helplessness (feigned or genuine) keeps them 'safe' will use more 'help me' expressions.

A child who learns to feel safest when in control of others (bullying or dominating) will habituate those behaviours. **Our job is not to judge what is right or wrong. It is simply to guide children towards a wider range of appropriate responses than they may currently perceive available.** We can do the same for ourselves as adults too.

As well as eliciting (drawing out) and benefiting from the emotional responses of other people, a child soon learns to **predict** responses in others. Neural patterns form familiar rhythms, and the brain likes rhythm.

Predicting patterns of behaviour helps to keep the Reptilian Brain feeling calm.

Predicting behaviour in others requires an ability to scan a wide range of sensory information (voice tone, fluidity of body movement, expressive sounds, or facial expressions) to help prepare useful responses.

For example, an adult might say 'no' and the child can feel safe if the adult's body, face and voice tone all express the same 'congruence' (consistency or harmony). On the other hand, an 'incongruent' adult saying *'no'* might trigger the child's Reptilian Brain to become alarmed, since it is *perceiving* mixed sensory messages and cannot safely predict what will happen next.

On a personal note, I remember one of my sons, who was aged around five at the time, would say to me, *"mummy you don't mean that",* to which I

41

would reply, *"listen to my words, of course I mean it"*. Out of the mouths of babes, as they say... I was trying to communicate with his Thinking Mind, but actually he was perceiving me through his lower brain and making a decision about how safe he felt based on my state of congruence.

With sensory information cascading through the whole brain at all times, the aim of this book is to help you to identify which brain 'part' to engage first in order to maximise communication. The Mammalian Brain holds simple clues.

Without the Thinking Mind engaged, our lower (Reptilian) and middle (Mammalian) **unconscious** brains are very animal-like, *sensing* safety, hostility, threat, a suitable mate, a suitable enemy etc., which is why we need executive guidance and rational thinking from the *prefrontal cortex* (next chapter) to help us to interpret what our nervous system is **receiving** and **processing**.

Electro-magnetic frequencies (EMFs) are now common technological parlance, and since all humans emit a measurable electro-magnetic chemistry into the field that surrounds the body, our brains and bodies are constantly **transmitting** massive amounts of electro-chemical information, just as all living organisms do.

Kids naturally tune into the signals of valuable Survive/Thrive information being non-consciously shared with our social group. Many adults tune this out or misinterpret it, both of which can seriously hamper long-term wellbeing.

Emotions amplify our state and we each have a personal electro-magnetic frequency (EMF) that transmits this information, as illustrated in this diagram.

42

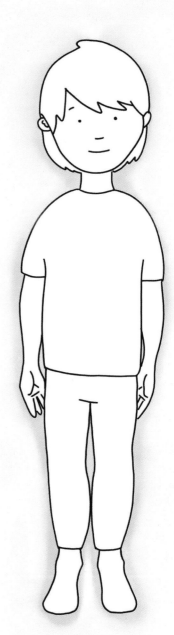

Think about the 'feeling' you get from being around:

o happy, joyful, excited people

o miserable, moaning, critical people

o angry, bitter, nasty people

It's easy to become attracted to someone who is 'feeling' the same as you (we feel safest in a pack), or who feels how you want to feel (safe). It's also easy keep away from someone you don't like the feel of.

I find that a lot of kids having trouble with their behaviour at school are bundled into groups of similarly agitated, stressed brains, where sparks literally fly. Or they live in homes which are like non-verbal battlefields.

Many people complain that they are affected by the feelings of others. People who are perceived as particularly 'sensitive' are usually those who feel overwhelmed when in contact with strong EMFs they do not like. That's not a bad thing, it's just misunderstood.

Resilience comes from being able to be present with any 'feeling' and not be jerked by it. We need to teach children how to manage their own EMFs and how to establish a different way to interpret the feeling by building, maintaining and exuding emotions of Thrive.

This is not only good for the individual, it also contributes to a better-quality world.

Happy Brain™ bases **resilience in the Mammalian Brain** because it is the key balancer of sensory information. From here, we go:

o **Downstairs** to the Reptilian Brain; '*does this feeling mean I am safe?*'

o **Upstairs** to the Thinking Mind; '*what else might this feeling mean?*'

ADAPTING

Children are naturally adept at social bonding and easily take on the emotions, behaviours, opinions and mannerisms of their peers and dominant social group, unconsciously aware that presenting themselves as similar/same, means they blend in.

It is a great survival strategy to feel and behave the same as others, since people like people who are the same as them (this equals safe and predictable). You will notice that standing out from the crowd or being different in some way can trigger great stress. It can also signal a '*please notice me*' stress pattern, which we will discuss more in later chapters.

I like the analogy that emotions are like 'glue' that waymarks what a brain has learned to consider is valuable enough to either seek more of, or to avoid. Both waymarks influence behaviour. All waymarks and therefore behaviours can be overlaid, toughened, removed, flaked or softened.

A child being kind to others may experience feeling good when praised by a significant adult and seek to repeat the feeling, setting up a pattern of reward.

The same child can feel uncomfortable when asking a question in class one day; setting up an emotional flag to *avoid this behaviour* in future.

Experience builds the neurological map and emotions mark importance flags or anchors into the map so that next time a similar experience is being sensed, emotions tell us whether to move towards or away from the stimulus.

As a mind experiment for you, think of something (any task) you want to do that, when you think of it, triggers a 'low' emotional feeling. Now think of something (any task) you want to do

43

that triggers a 'high' emotional feeling. Bear in mind how each of the above feels when you read on, because we're now scratching the surface of 'how' people motivate themselves.

Motivation comes from a feeling. Most people are motivated to get away from unpleasant feelings and move towards nice feelings.

EMOTIONS FLOW

Many, many emotions continually ebb and flow in response to daily life, mostly undetected since much of our day may seem unremarkable to the brain. Occasionally, reactions that are of a notably high or low **intensity** alert a certain chemical glue to 'catch' sensory information as of perceived importance. To represent the ebb and flow of emotional states, I think of an undulating wave form to represent the daily flow of emotional highs and lows. Use your hand to gesture:

- o   A flow of highs and lows
- o   An infinity symbol

Keep this flowing in mind as you help yourself and others to manage emotions. When working with clients, I visualise where they are on this waveform so that I can help them to flow through to a more useful feeling. **Flowing *out of* unresourceful feelings and *into* the most useful ones is key to resilience.**

Withholding emotion

A child falling over and hurting themselves when playing alone will almost always hold in their emotional expression until safely reunited with the social group. It's as if lower brain regions (Reptilian and Mammalian) don't want to reveal their vulnerability to would-be predators; delaying a cry for help could keep the child safe.

Just for a moment, think about that 'holding in' of emotion as an adult; all that energy building inside, just ready to explode. Many adults do this habitually. Withholding stress energy is really bad for health. As you saw in the last chapter, with this stress response, blood pressure increases, cholesterol and sugar levels rise, the heart rate increases, thinking capabilities nosedive, etc.

Holding onto these sensations of stress can cause physical and mental illness, often because emotional expression has been repressed. You've heard of a pressure cooker. How many adults come home from work and 'release' their emotional day through art, music, sport, dance? Or to their family? Or in the pub? *Or hold it in?*

The child who fell over in the playground, once safe at home, can hopefully offload their full emotional expression and re-set quickly. In doing so, they can also build more 'association' data for their neurological map, building an algorithm connected to the emotion, for example:

Expressing emotion = ice cream / cuddles / ridicule / distraction / punishment / etc.

Adult algorithms are not so dissimilar, although the associations may also include alcohol, drugs, sex, TV, food etc.

Chasing good emotions

21st Century western society's marketing machine drives vast economic success by selling us products that will make us feel good. You can easily buy yourself an instant feel good through altering your appearance, acquiring material signs of wealth, denoting social status through acquaintances (and now social media). **Marketers tell us** what to wear, eat, drink and how to behave, which they sell to us through our emotional

44

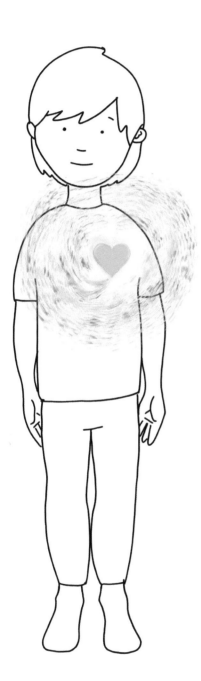

brain (*stop feeling ugly, sad and lonely – all you need to do is buy this and you will feel popular, young and sexy; you need this...*).

It's so easy to be passive recipients of the global marketing machine, bombarded by strong sensory stimuli through modern technologies. **We are encouraged to chase good feelings and fear bad feelings,** which has little to do with the products or services being touted. The modern age confuses our Mammalian Brain because neurologically we are supposed to balance the ebb and flow of a *variety of feelings*.

I believe we should also be careful not to teach children to fear or avoid so-called 'bad' emotional feelings because that interferes with our natural state, as well as triggering a spiral of fear-based worries, e.g. *'I must only say positive things, I mustn't say anything that could offend someone...'*

I also think it is folly to teach children to seek only so-called 'good' feelings, because:

o So-called 'bad' feelings can be an important feedback mechanism to move away from making stupid decisions.

o We can always find short cuts to good feelings (sugar, drugs, alcohol, risk taking, social approval ...)

o Passive 'taking' or 'receiving' only good feelings sets up dependency.

We want to teach the brain how to organise thoughts, feelings and behaviours that *work towards something **and then** are suitably rewarded.*

Balance is the key once more, and we are aiming to build emotional databases that have **experienced a wide range of feelings** with the ability to associate a 'useful' emotion to a clear goal.

45

Note: Many people – especially children, find it easier to talk about emotions as being the language and energy of the heart, which emits its own powerful and measurable electro-magnetic frequency, as illustrated in this diagram.

Activity: Kitty Thumb

Have your child (or inner child) imagine their thumb as a soft, purring, calm cat and talk them through this script:

Look at your left-hand thumb and move it around softly and slowly. Imagine it as your personal kitty. What's its name? Describe the (imagined) softness and texture of its fur. Can you imagine the sound of it purring?

Now with your right hand, gently stroke and cuddle the thumb until it is ready to curl up inside the palm of your left hand. Now softly fold your left-hand fingers around it and let it rest. Feel soft calmness in your left hand spreading up through your left arm, across your shoulders and down into your right palm. Wait until the right palm is a copycat and also feels calm.

Sometimes, when we get angry or sad, the kitty 'flips out' from its sleepy place and suddenly all your fingers spread out like a cat's claws. Go ahead and make this happen – feel the stiffness of the stress reaction. You probably notice your shoulders feel tense too, right? And the right palm – how does that feel now?

If you stayed tense like that, your body would become unwell and your mind would become unhappy, so we need to train ourselves to return to the nice, soft feeling of calm.

Here's how: give some kindness and attention to the kitty thumb and help it return to feeling soft and cuddly by looking at it with smiling eyes and moving it around softly and slowly. Whisper its name (out loud or inside your mind). Gently feel the softness and texture of its fur. Can you hear it purring yet?

Now with your right hand, gently stroke and cuddle the thumb until it is ready to curl up inside the palm of your left hand. Now softly fold your fingers around it and let it rest.

46

HELP CHILDREN DO SOMETHING DIFFERENT WITH THEIR EMOTIONS

Research suggests that people with perceived 'good' mental health are more able to identify, name and express a range of emotional states than those with poorer mental health, but for some who have been conditioned to withhold emotional expression, this can be difficult.

I find imagery helps to tune into emotions and I use the Happy Brain™ Perceived Emotion Scale (PES) as a fun tool to help explore and express shifting emotional states without the complication of language. It also presupposes to children that at least 10 emotional responses are routine and 'normal'. I use this scale with adults too - often the most serious grown-ups need a different level of engagement than taking themselves too seriously. **The emotional brain is playful!**

Since most humans have 10 moving digits, we can connect (metaphorically or with a sticker) each of these emotions to a finger/thumb. You now have 10 emotions to move, so practice, experience and express their fluidity. I might ask a child which 'face' on the PES best represents how they are feeling right now, and which is the feeling they would rather have instead (providing them with somewhere to aim their emotional flow).

The Happy Brain™ coaching kit has 30 different emotional representations, each printed onto palm-sized discs with a mirror on the other side. There are so many games to play with emotions like these, each teaching children that fluidity and range of emotional expression is useful.

For example, finding how someone is associating particular feelings to specific aspects of their life. I might ask *'so the last time you felt like* [number 8, say] *what was happening? How and where did you feel those feelings in your body?'*

This builds on what we learned in the last chapter and leads into the skills and knowledge to come. The gold star goes to adults who can effortlessly generate spontaneous laughter using the PES – a wonderful chemical bathe in cleansing brain juice and essential to all.

47

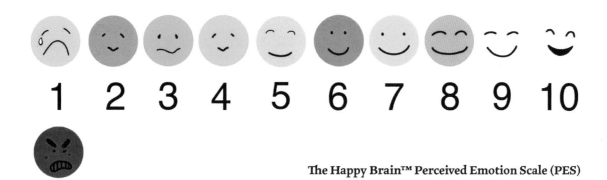

The Happy Brain™ Perceived Emotion Scale (PES)

Evaluation notes: Happy Brain™ Assistant during Year 3 workshop

At first break, a few of the kids stayed back in the classroom. Kay talked with a boy, and I saw a girl sitting in the corner of the room almost crying, with her friend looking concerned next to her. I went over and asked if she was ok. We talked about some things that were bothering her that day, and when I asked her to tell me how she was feeling, she (unprompted) looked around and found a PES on a nearby table and pointed to 1 or 2. I was surprised that she wanted to use the scale, because we hadn't really done too much work with it yet. She couldn't say how she was feeling, and when she tried, she could only say things like "I just feel sick". I thought how useful the scale can be in situations like this, to get a sense of what a kid is feeling, when they can't find the words to describe their feelings.

Towards the end of the day, I sat with two kids, a girl and a boy, who had headaches. I asked them to find where the pain started, how it moved and give it a colour (we had already done 'spinning'-type exercises with the class). I then asked the kids to slow down the movement and reverse it. I then got them to give it a different colour. After a while, I asked them how their headaches were, on a scale 1-10 (1=worst, 10=feeling best). The boy said that his had improved to a 6. He said it still hurt, but felt a little bit better than when we started. I asked him to continue, and after a little while asked him again. This time he said it had improved to 9.

The girl said she still felt really bad, so I tried another activity. I got them to imagine how they feel when they feel really relaxed but happy. I asked them to feel how it would feel and sit in that relaxed position. The girl said she was relaxed and happy in the bath, and so she slid down in her chair as if she was in the bath. The boy chose playing on his X-box, so he sat leaning forward, 'holding' the controls and 'looking' at the screen. Both kids visibly changed when doing this, especially the girl, who was now smiling and joking.

I asked them where this feeling of being relaxed and happy started, how it moved and what colour it would have. I then asked them to keep looping this good feeling through the point where the headache feeling was. The girl seemed to be doing ok with this, but the boy said that this actually made his head hurt more! I think he said his pain was now at a 4. So, I asked him to remember what he did to make it get up to a 9 and to keep doing that.

THINK AGAIN

Opening a parent coaching session one day, I ambiguously asked them *'so how are things with X [child]?'* and after 12 minutes of negative reporting, doom and gloom, describing only what they didn't like about their child's behaviours, I noted that both parents looked thoroughly miserable. So, to set an example of 'balance', I asked them to spend the following 12 minutes talking only about all the positive experiences, thoughts and feelings they could associate to their child.

They stumbled after a few minutes. I explained to them this was not a trap or criticism, just a perfect opportunity to learn how they had become 'weighed down' by their own habitual patterns of thinking about their child and their **dominant**

48

emotional associations to him. They now had a choice, to stick with their auto-pilot old patterns of associating their child with their feelings of unhappiness, or to choose to build new patterns of resilience. Shocked, but grateful to realise this, they chose to build new patterns that would help the whole family unit thrive.

ANCHORS

Have you ever been busy doing nothing when suddenly your ears tuned into a song playing in the background, and instantly you felt transported back to your teenage years?

Your brain *heard* the soundwaves and recognised the *pattern* that *triggered* a neurological *code* for something significant that made this memorable.

NLP calls this an 'anchor', because the sensory experience (e.g. sound) has been **associated** to other sensory experiences within the memory and glued with a strong feeling. The memory can be triggered at any time, by a splinter of sensory detail. Recently, I caught a whiff of a perfume I wore at the time of my divorce, decades ago, and suddenly my brain offered: 'here is your memory'.

Anchors provide a fast track to 'remember' useful things like a dog that bites, a plant that poisons, or a piece of music that relaxes.

We can build anchors on purpose too, by being aware of the associations we are forming naturally and practising the ones that build our capacity to thrive

Sadly, anchors that trigger distress are so often encoded accidentally in childhood. For example, the teacher saying you are hopeless at maths or cannot draw. If only we paid more attention to the evolving neurological map of children so we could strengthen useful anchors and weaken the anchors that might limit future performances.

BALANCE

I consciously noted the importance of balancing a child's emotional associations 25 years ago, when my son came home from school with a piece of creative writing entitled '*the saddest day of my life*'.

While I'm the first to acknowledge the importance of emotional expression, there had been no teaching of balance to his state and my 8-year-old had become immersed in an hour of great sadness focusing on the memory of our pet cat being run over. This well-meaning activity also had the potential for deep upset in class and potentially associating the child's feelings of sadness to the classroom.

Fortunately, I was able to avert the sad memory looping (rumination) by instinctively re-directing my child's attention towards happy memories of our pet.

Sadly, not all children get to learn how to move **through a sad feeling into a happy feeling** like this, and they can end up stuck in sadness or anger that triggers a Stress reaction.

We need to think about how we are helping or hindering children's neurological patterns; if you are going to ask about sad things, remember to then take the conversation towards happy feelings (remembered, present or imagined), thus embedding a powerful self-managing pattern of emotional resilience. As we will see in the next chapter, our brains make the smartest decisions about behaviour when bathed in Thrive chemistry. Let's build the blueprint for this.

49

GATHERING INFORMATION THROUGH PLAY

A fun activity I use with kids is called **happy-sad senses,** where they get to record what they currently associate with each of their 5 primary senses. This helps me to gather useful information, so in a moment we'll look at the types of associations that may or may not be useful to the child's ability to Thrive. This activity can also be played with a 'timeline spinning arrow' that orientates attention through time to past – present – future, to help children understand the difference between emotionally encoded experiences that are:

- o Real (remembered)
- o Real (present and verifiable by others)
- o Imaginary (future)

Notice this activity asks for a balance of happy – sad feelings.

	I like lookin at my hamster		My dead hamster Poppy
	I like Smelling chocalate cake		My hamsters wee + pumps
	I like hearing my cat Purring		People hammering
	My big fluffy soft cat		Mad I hate touching
	Chocalate		carrots

In the first example above, the sensory information and emotional reference comes entirely from memory with no present sensory experience being referenced. And just by thinking about these things, the child will have accessed feelings because the associations run automatically.

In the second example (below), we might wonder at *'no Christmas presents', 'no money' 'no sweetie tin.'*

To be missing, these things of high value have firstly been **imagined as available** (= happy emotional chemistry), and then **imagined as being taken away** by someone (= sad emotional chemistry).

That's a lot of *confusing brain energy*, a lot of *chaotic neural pathways connecting through strong high/low emotional chemistry*. A perfect example of *inadvertent brain training that sets up patterns of anxiety.*

Can you see how the 8-year-old child filling in the paper below is moving out of sensory-based information and into their opinions of the world?

We might wonder what they meant by *'Oprah bad comments'* because it would seem this child is already forming patterns of reacting to their 'internal' emotional map because the sad feeling is being triggered by a 'thought' alone.

Swimming pool diving lessons	no christmas presents no money no sweety tin	
Chocolate candy crocets floss	poo fish Smelly toilets pump	
comlement concert	opra Bad coments Screeming fire work	
play dough pastry	bones wax bare bum	
crocets Bacon chocolate	Fish Jelly mouse wooster souce	

In the third example (below), the child is expressing strong emotions of love and hate.

Given that many adults can only oscillate between extreme emotions rather than a range of expressions, I'd be inclined by this to play-act a range of balancing emotions to build patterns of tolerance (rather than patterns of reaction) to the outside world.

Such strength of emotional reaction in this example suggests this child is not in their 'Thrive' brain and is already limiting their learning abilities in class.

Can you see the expression of wanting/needing people to be kind 'to' them in this example, and avoiding people who shout? Beliefs like this deplete resilience. A resilient child stays stable regardless of the whirlwinds of other people's behaviours. When I see, hear or feel a strong emotional reaction, the questions on my mind are:

- o   What is the intention of the emotion (self-expression or receive attention)?
- o   Whose attention is being engaged (and is it consciously or unconsciously)?
- o   How does the emotion help or hinder behaviour?
- o   How does the emotion help or hinder thinking?
- o   Is the emotion powering Thrive, or Survive?
- o   What emotions are needed to re-balance and drive Thrive?

These questions are on my mind so that I can get more information and build in the necessary resources through further play without addressing them directly.

53

Activity: Still Point

This simple activity helps people to discover more about their sense of personal boundaries and better perceive the boundaries of others.

I often find that exploration of 'boundaries' provides people with insights about their perceived limitations and interaction with others. Hula hoops (the plastic hoops, not the savoury snacks...) are my favourite teaching prop. I carry all sizes and colours almost everywhere I go and have 101 ways to use them.

Stand in the centre of a hula hoop, it may be on the ground or held around the hips.

This is your Still Point, your 'centre'. Sense the space between your physical body and the edges of the hoop. This is your personal space.

Many people can relate to this as their field of energy, emitted by mind and body electro-magnetic chemistry (the EMF we explored earlier). Be absolutely balanced in the centre of your world.

Stand straight and symmetrical with feet slightly apart. Keep your shoulders rolled back and head tall. Breathe as you would for Balloon Breathing.

Activity: Power Up - feel powerful and strong from the inside

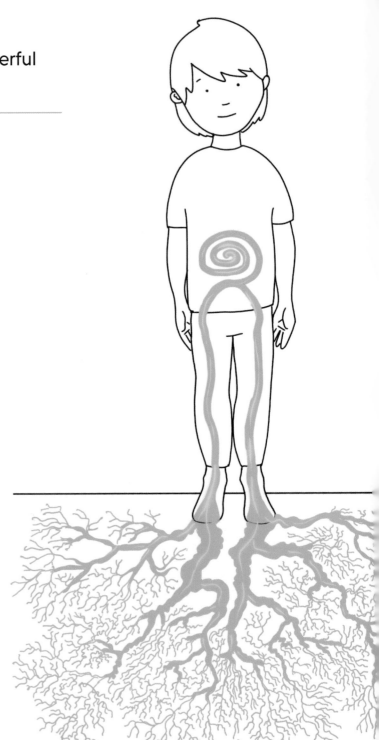

Place your right thumb over your tummy button and cup your hand to rest on your tummy beneath it. In martial arts, this area is often called your centre of energy; you can think of it a bit like your **personal power pack.**

Keep concentrating on this power pack until you feel either the palms of your hand tingling or warmth inside your tummy. Notice how your personal power energy feels and decide how to make it stronger, for example changing the direction, colour, or sound of it, as you did in Spinning Feelings. Spread strong feelings throughout your whole body.

Once the wave of energy and power reaches your feet, imagine it travelling down into the ground and growing roots – strong roots that anchor you and make you feel very stable.

Now focus on the Still Point of your balance. Have someone call you names and tune into the 'feelings' that change if someone says to you *'you're really smart'* or *'you're really stupid'*. And naturally (intuitively) sway or move towards or away from the words being spoken.

After you **feel the pull or push** of whatever words are spoken, return to the centre of your sphere and feel your control and strength in this centre.

Anecdote

I remember a corporate client who was by any standards a visually stunning model lookalike, only she moved physically in a way that suggested she was emotionally unsettled, if not 'all over the place'. I chose her to help me demonstrate this technique because of her visibly shifting physiology and asked her buddies in the group to 'feed' her compliments (that were of value to her) including *'you're really beautiful'* whereby she stood still, tall and centred.

Next, they hurled insults like *'you're really ugly'* and despite knowing that this was just a game, her emotions reacted, producing bodily movements that fluctuated back and forth like a ship in stormy waters. I had one of her colleagues 'coach' her to re-balance herself until she could do it solo, adding a soft voice (inside her mind) *'I'm still and I am calm'* to help remind her how to connect to her Powering Up sensations. She was teaching her nervous system to re-balance after a whirlwind and teaching her emotional brain to self-adjust.

This is one of my favourite techniques to teach children who feel they are being bullied but are actually just unable to self-manage feelings. I encourage them to visualise where their 'personal power' is; inside or outside a hula hoop; still point or oscillating; inside the body chaos or direction. And so on.

Note: Emotional rewards
The purpose of the exercises above is to train the brain to be aware of the qualities of 'internal' power and 'external' power.

Feeling good because someone is being kind to you is a natural thing.
Feeling good **only** when someone is kind to you sets up unhealthy patterns:
   o   Seeking attention in order to feel good
   o   Feeling hurt or offended when people don't make you feel good

Too many people give away their emotional stability to the outside world.

55

BELIEFS

Beliefs are simply neural codes that have become valued over time and are waymarked by strong emotions. A person's beliefs can be heard as language patterns such as *'everyone...' 'always...' 'no-one...'* as in *'he always shouts'* or *'she is never kind'*.

These patterns of thought and feeling are like shortcuts in the neurological map and become **autopilot programmes**. This is the **Programming** part of Neuro Linguistic Programming.

Many beliefs are *useful*, some are *not*. Think about **beliefs** as neural pathways that have fired and wired together and teamed up with other, similar pathways, super-bonded together by strong emotions.

Such powerful, super-bonded connections give rise to a sense of certainty due to the intensity of sensations and frequency of being accessed.

Beliefs drive decision-making, and children are building a foundation of beliefs that will guide them through life.

Resilience involves having the ability to modify outdated beliefs.

Beliefs are easily formed

Can you absolutely predict, with certainty, someone's reaction to a spider? If so, you are privy to their encoded 'programme' for reacting to spiders.

If you can't predict with certainty, then you may be able to hazard a guess as to their response, based on what you may have observed as 'patterns' of their previous behaviours.

To help us to understand this a bit more, let's look at the process of encoding a spider programme which (probably) began with an early encounter during childhood:

o Scenario 1: The infant's instinct to explore through all senses resulted in (spider) smelling/tasting disgusting and their nervous system flagged that as a code:
See-smell-taste > move away = preparing/ initialising a potential pattern for future reference.

o Scenario 2: A bite from the spider caused a pain signal inside the nervous system that needed adult attention:
Cry > seek safety >remember the sensory experience > avoid in future = installing a code for future reference.

o Scenario 3: The sound of shrieking from another human hijacked the nervous system's instinct for survival and all sensory experience of that moment in time became encoded and prioritised in the neurological map:
*Hear shriek = threat to survival = avoid at all costs = **encoding a priority programme to autopilot.***

Note: there are many potential scenarios here, but you get the idea of how senses and emotions are involved in creating programmes within the brain.

The point here is not about spiders (of course, we all want to remain safe and gather relevant information, e.g. which are dangerous and which are harmless); we want our children's neurological *response potential* to be flexible so that in future they may choose to scream, run, laugh, ignore, stamp on it, explore it, be curious. etc.

We want to build their resilience so they can respond with choice, not react to their autopilot for the rest of their lives, screaming hysterically whenever a spider enters the room.

Beliefs are formed as patterns of high value in the neurological map:

o   In the lower, Reptilian Brain over time and use (frequency)

o   In the middle, Mammalian Brain with high emotion (intensity)

o   Early detection of beliefs – useful and non-useful - presents opportunities for us to build upon, ie. *"yes, you should avoid that poisonous spider, so let's find out more so we can learn about different types of spiders".*

We can help deconstruct and change the encoding that supports a belief like 'all spiders are terrifying' and instead give the brain a different way to *respond* rather than *react*.

An NLP technique called *changing submodalities* is a simple and effective way to alter the sensory encoding in relation to the emotional reaction. This technique gathers information about the 'encoding' by conversationally eliciting the *submodalities* (sensory components) of a behaviour, and then deliberately changes the brain's neural connections by 'changing' the submodalities.

We always want the brain to have a more useful direction to be heading in, and this is one way of doing it. We will practise this later.

This brings us to being influenced by adult beliefs; a major problem when working with children since they are primed (for good survival reasons) to imprint the beliefs of significant adults.

Check out the Rosenthal Experiment *(Rosenthal and Jacobsen, 1968)*, a psychological experiment where children's classroom performances – good and bad - were shown to directly mirror the teachers' 'expectations', i.e. their beliefs about the children. In this randomised study, children who were deemed either 'slow' or 'smart' performed academically in accordance with their teachers' expectations. This has subsequently been termed *'the expectancy effect'* and highlights the problems some children face when labelled.

You can set up your own similar enquiry:

o   What do you believe about yourself and your child?

o   What if you were right about that?

o   What if you were wrong about that?

o   How do your beliefs about yourself support your Thrive Drive?

o   How do your beliefs about your child support their opportunities to Thrive?

57

Evaluation note: Happy brain™ Assistant during Year 3 workshop

As soon as I sat down at the back, the class 3 teacher who was observing told me that this was a 'difficult' class, and that you could tell this because the kids weren't being very quiet, and you could hear background murmuring around the classroom.

IMAGINATION

Our brain continually receives sensory fragments which it 'processes' by connecting them in different ways through billions of neural pathways. Regularly used connections become what we call *memories*, and new connections are what we call *imagination*.

Imagination pervades every aspect of our internal and external worlds where shape, sound, colour, form and limitless possibilities are crafted from fragments of sensory experiences.

Using imagination helps athletes to mentally rehearse their neurological map to build strong pathways for focused success. Once the pathways are imagined and rehearsed, the brain has a new way to operate because it has formed a memory for the future.

Imagination can also be misused and hoodwink people into mentally rehearsing an instant feel-good through food, alcohol, drugs, etc. Sometimes, we have to teach people to keep their imagination running forward further in time so that they can imagine the consequences of their behaviours.

Our brains have the ability to produce amazing psychedelic experiences, through sleep dreams or daydreams, or by deliberately taking control of our internal worlds. I love to teach teenagers the power of their imagination to produce amazing imagery with surround sounds and stunningly powerful states of choice. When they learn how to do this through hypnosis and then self-hypnosis, they are empowered to make better decisions about the temptations of illegal mind-altering substances. Emotions power imagination and emotional feelings are addictive.

Some people spend their days imagining all sorts of terrible things that never happened or will never happen, generating powerful survival feelings that can weirdly become comforting in their familiarity.

Likewise, some people spend their days lost in a fantasy that stops them functioning in the real world. We have to help young people take control of their imagination and use it to Thrive.

Imagination is a power tool for resilience.

Visualisation is a commonly used term for powering up the sensory fragments within a neurological map – with a purpose. Did you know that some of the world's greatest genius minds have shared this ability to visualise? Leonardo Da Vinci and Isaac Newton are noted for their ability to harness the potential of the brain's right hemisphere and unconscious mind to nurture 'whole brain' thinking. It is said that the theory of relativity was born from a dreamlike fantasy of riding a beam of light around the universe.

Nikola Tesla's 19th Century discovery of alternating current begins like most typical invention stories. He scrutinised the theories, the mechanics, and every minute detail. Finally, he built the first motor, and then allowed it to run continuously for three months. One of the things that is remarkable about Tesla is that the AC model he built and tested for three months was *inside* his head. When he finally built his first physical prototype, it worked without fail. As he knew it would - thanks to visualisation.

The top golfer Tiger Woods first visualised winning the US Masters when he was 12, and he still uses this visualisation technique today to dominate his sport. Team GB's Olympic successes have also been largely credited to the practice of visualisation, and this is now an integral part of sports psychology.

The list goes on with successful people who have accredited their success to visualisation. They include Martin Luther King Jr, Thomas Edison, Michael Jordan, Winston Churchill, Beethoven, Napoleon, Carl Lewis, Alexander Graham Bell, and more.

Activity: Remember, remember

As an introduction to your creative superpowers, try this mind experiment...

Remember one particularly happy childhood day. As you are doing this, remember that your brain is searching through millions of neural patterns to fit this request; filtering for happy emotions, early life experience, and daytime sensory modalities (channels of information).
Note: I am directing your attention to something that feels good. More about that later...

Now as you access whatever was perceived and encoded in your nervous system at some moment in the past, what do you recall? In your memory, what did you see, hear, touch, smell, taste, and how did you move, balance and feel inside?

I'm wondering about the finer distinctions of your memory; did your brain store the information in colour or black and white? Is the memory held still like a photograph, or moving like a movie?

Are the sounds in your memory stereo, mono or surround sound? What are the types of fragrances and odours? Do your taste buds linger salty or sweet? What about the textures and temperature in your memory?

NLP calls this *accessing your submodalities* (the finer distinctions of sensory modalities we touched on a few pages ago). We use this skill to self-manage emotions because the quality of the sounds and images is linked to an emotional charge. Therefore, if you change one, you change the other.

For example, switch back and forth between seeing yourself in the memory, and looking through your own eyes. How do you feel differently?

How much can you adjust the volume of sounds? Remember, we practised some of these sensory channel techniques in the last chapter.

Now add something else imaginary to that memory that will make you smile even more. Do it on purpose to increase the good feelings associated with your memory. How about adding the sound of giggles from another human, or picking up a giant seashell, or building a triple decker sandwich, or deep diving with mermaids.

This process is about learning to drive your Happy Brain™, on purpose. What a delicious bedtime treat for yourself or for a child!

Of course, you know the reverse is also true - some people practise recalling sad memories or making scary imaginations; a gross misuse of imagination which rehearses a worry pattern that builds stress chemistry and hoodwinks the brain into waymarking those feelings as being important...

59

MIND MAGIC

Young children are especially good at solving problems using mind magic techniques. Recently, a 5-year old client invented an imaginary unicorn that could torpedo her recurrent nightmare, blasting the movie clear out of the night. Now that's a smart use of imagination!

I love watching a child light up with delight when they imagine a solution to their current difficulty that puts them in the driving seat and allows them to feel back in control.

Only the parents will ask, *'but why is she having the nightmare, what is wrong with her?'*... or *'but she needs me to reassure her and sleep in her bed'*... rather than teaching the child how to self-manage natural fears and set up neurological patterns of resilience by using imagination to find new neural connections.

I remember beginning a Year 5 Happy Brain™ workshop in the original 2010 project by having each child choose a palm-sized emoticon disc. Throughout the morning (and at every opportunity) I had the children associate (*anchor*) oodles of happy feelings to their personalised laminated emotion disc.

By the afternoon, we were ready to set up a *'magic circle'* where each child carefully placed their happy feeling discs inside a large and particularly sparkly hula hoop.

Engaging in a bit of theatre and drama to triple their excitement around **'all the happiness of the class now resting inside our magic hoop...'** each child took turns to step into this magic circle of extraordinary class happiness.

Their anticipation was palpable and I chose the quietest, least confident child to step inside the hoop first - *"one step at a time, not too fast, oh my, you are going to share all the class happiness between you, woowwwwww ..."*

I saw, heard, felt, the thrill of this exercise that was teaching their neurology something wonderful; a feeling (physiological sensation powerful enough to be called an emotion) that we could connect by visualisation to a future memory, like sitting a test.

Thrive brains take a thrive-power feeling to overpower a stress-power feeling!

Only the teacher said, *'well that wasn't very magic, was it..?'* But the teacher didn't understand 'how' this works, despite me explaining that the 'naughty chair' works the same system in reverse by setting up lots of sad feelings from every child in class.

Case Study: Wrap Trap

Joel was 14 when his distraught parents asked for help. They had discovered he was looking at 'inappropriate' content on YouTube.

The parents had tried talking to their son through their intelligent and compassionate family values. To no avail - the allure of the 'inappropriate content' appeared unbreakable.

Joel had become obsessed, or so it seemed. Despite his parents having confiscated his phone, blocked his access to the internet and withdrawn other privileges, he kept discovering new ways around the sanctions. Joel's parents feared the worst; they ran their imaginations fast-forward to having a deviant, misogynist adult son with a sexual fetish.

Joel has a diagnosis of Asperger Syndrome, and although he was 14 years old at this time, he had academic and social assessments that put him at around 12 years of age.

Fortunately, I had worked with this family before, so it was easy to quickly calm the mum and introduce some 'possibility' into her thinking. *"It is possible, isn't it, that Joel's brain could make new connections and break old ones..?"* I probed.

"Please, just hypnotise him!" she pleaded.

But he appeared quite hypnotised already - by the internet - and I had some investigation and calibration to be getting on with. So, Joel, my dog Oscar and I settled into a game of Snakes and Ladders.

This game is one of my tried and trusted activities for 1:1 work with young people. Trying to win the game is a fun process for re-directing kids' attention, setting up positive neurochemistry (dopamine and acetylcholine in particular are released when there is chance/novelty involved), thus encouraging whole-brain activity.

We did not include Oscar in our battle to win, but we did rely on him as a mood setter; a furry friend to pat, stroke, and generally induce happy feelings (people make better decisions when they are feeling good...).

Apart from the obvious rules of Snakes and Ladders, our additions to the game were:

o Landing on a snake's head = **tell** the other person (or Oscar the dog) something that bothers you.

o Landing at the foot of a ladder = **ask** the other person (or Oscar the dog) something you'd like to know more about.

Note: For some children and young people, particularly those on the ASD spectrum, talking to a dog feels easier than talking to a human.

Our fun exchanges of 'ask' and 'tell' were many and varied, until Joel suddenly announced that he had 'problems growing up' and how he wished he was 11 or 12 again because, he said, his life was now *'ruined'*!

"Ruined?" I exclaimed.

"Yes, ruined," he replied, with certainty.

"Oh wow, Oscar, Joel's life is ruined," I said to the dog, involving him to add another layer of communication and slow it all down.

Joel began to look anxious; he began fidgeting and his breathing quickened.

"Oscar looks a little upset at the idea your life is ruined Joel, so before we carry on, will you remind him how to do Balloon Breathing and calm him down?"

61

Remember, Balloon Breathing is the activity from our Happy Brain™ Calm Confidence kit which we practised in Chapter 1. This technique de-activates the sympathetic nervous system and brings a sense of calm. I held Oscar on my lap, exaggerating his rib expansion to show Joel how to slowly breathe. By 'teaching' Oscar to balloon breathe, he had to do it for himself, and once we synchronised a slower breathing rhythm, everyone's breathing became calmer.

This perfectly interrupted Joel's state of worry and he became calmer, so I continued: *"Sorry Joel, I didn't mean to interrupt you, but thank you for helping Oscar – you were telling us that your life was ruined. That sounds horrid, how come?"*

*"Because of the inappropriate videos **I am possessed by.**"* He sighed, sounding resigned to believing this as a truth. Note: 'Possessed' seemed a suitable word as he went on to describe his nightmares and worries. He really was at an impasse.

Taking this information (his reality) at face value, with no emotional attachment or response, I began to dig for more information. If you are familiar with NLP, you will know that the Meta Model provides a superb structure for gathering good quality information, especially when the questions are 'softened' with Milton language.

Still playing Snakes and Ladders as a pace keeper, Joel gradually revealed several parts to the problem as he perceived it:

o His life was ruined due to being barred from using the internet.

o His life was ruined because his parents would never trust him again.

o His life was ruined because since his mind became infected 2 years ago, he constantly felt terrified and had frequent nightmares.

Whilst it is rarely necessary for us to know the 'content' of a problem, I decided to investigate what it was that Joel believed had *infected* him, *possessed* him, and apparently *ruined* his life.

The 'inappropriate content' he had found himself attached to turned out to be a series of YouTube videos of middle-aged men catching pretty young girls and then 'wrapping' them in duct tape in a kidnap-like manner.

"How did you find this video, Joel?" I asked him, in a matter-of-fact voice.

He replied, *"I just love rap music."*

Again, listening to his words, literally, the ambiguity (wrapping / rapping) exploded a whole new set of possibilities, and sure enough, it soon transpired that Joel had quite innocently been looking up RAP videos on the Internet when inadvertently he had discovered WRAP threads of a different nature. And, to complicate matters more, his search engine algorithm would have had the word 'warp' logged in it, since his favourite Doctor Who theme could be found on a YouTube music channel called Warp Zone.

So, we had uncovered the link between Rap-Wrap-Warp …

Now I was beginning to make some sense of the jigsaw pieces that had, until now, mis-joined into a confusing picture.

The mystery unravelled as Joel explained how, two years previously, when he was around 12 years old and searching for *rap* music videos on YouTube, he had accidentally discovered those inappropriate videos of pretty girls being wrapped and bound. He became terrified by the idea that this was what all adults did, and he himself would have to do this one day, or have it done to him. He became fixated with trying to understand and make some sense of it all.

62

Watching it over and over alongside other similar videos seemed his brain's way to make sense of it all, yet it also paralysed him and that was when the nightmares began. Nightmares that he would have to wrap up someone or be wrapped up himself.

Joel's brain was **receiving** sensory information for which he had no reference to help him **process** it or **act upon it.** He was indeed trapped.

Incidentally, his mum had previously reported that all Sellotape in the house seemed to disappear immediately she bought it. Now Joel confessed to binning it in terror!

Caught in a loop, Joel's disgust and fear of violence and kidnapping served to reinstate his very gentle nature and very real fear of growing up, if this was what was to come. His strongly developing values were now being compromised, not least by the fact that some of those girls had pretty faces that stirred a feeling of adolescent 'attraction'.

His parents discovered his obsession through the family computer browsing history and consequently he had his access to it severely restricted – at that time, no more YouTube. Now Joel was both devastated to lose access to YouTube music, yet also greatly relieved.

"At least I'm away from it all now," he sighed, filled with remorse, guilt, and sadness for having disappointed his parents. *"I've made a terrible mistake,"* he whispered.

I made the following observations to myself:

o Joel was able to express normal adolescent 'attraction/love' feelings towards females in general (e.g. a girl on the school bus).
o Joel showed no misogynistic tendencies.
o He felt spellbound by the videos.
o He was upset at the consequences of his actions.

o *Joel described his brain being 'infected' by what he had been watching.*
o *He believed he was not trustworthy enough to prevent it happening again.*

*Italics indicate where I decided to intervene.

More Snakes and Ladders 'ask and tell' exchanges enabled me to explain how those videos did not have to be part of his adulthood, and we explored a range of 'normal' adulthood behaviours for which he had some reference. By dismissing the videos as silly and sad, I began the process of offering some reassurance that his worst nightmares were truly unfounded. After checking that he did indeed want to be free of those images inside his mind, remembering Joel's language of 'being infected' was a great place to start the process of change.

We chatted about computers being infected with viruses and how easy it was these days to have the infection/virus wiped clean. He agreed that it was easily done.

"Fortunately," I explained, *"I know some fun and easy ways to wipe clean 'mind infections. It's called mind magic ...'*

After some more Balloon Breathing to speed his access to subconscious mind resources, I asked Joel to close his eyes and *'imagineer'* a **master control centre** inside his mind. As a Star Wars fan, he modelled his control centre like a Jedi spaceship, where he could pull levers, fire buttons and have surround-sound screens, speakers and a swivel chair.

By leading him through a creative visualisation, I had Joel recall a 'wrapping' image memory that he didn't like too much - not yet producing a huge stress response, as I was still teaching him how to use the power controls inside his brain.

Placing the image on the surround screen of his

63

64

Jedi spaceship, Joel's mind's eye found the button on his imaginary control panel that froze the moving image. Pulling a red lever, he had the picture '*Splat!*' against the windscreen of his spaceship, like a parking ticket on his dad's car. Now he could switch on the windscreen wipers, and as he watched he heard the disintegration of the picture.

"That was easy," he said.

We continued to play inside his imagination, recalling image after image, some on screens inside his spaceship and others placed as targets on enemy spaceships. One by one, the images that had infected his mind were destroyed through a series of explosions, shrinking, fading, smashing; all with powerful sound effects and a strong feeling of being in control.

Imagineering to 'change pictures and sounds' like this is an NLP technique; the results feel utterly magical and Joel was indeed flabbergasted when I asked him to recall those old scary images (note the linguistic presupposition of the past tense 'those *old* scary images', just to hedge my bets); no, they were gone and replaced by a blank screen. A successful anti-virus clean-up!

I asked Joel if his mind could now create an 'anti-virus app' that could place any scary images on his mind's screen before wiping them away, just like swiping his phone screen, or would his brain's control centre know just what to do should scary images ever emerge again in the future? This was both a double bind (an illusion of choice) and an example of future-pacing (projecting into the future) certainty that he

would be able to drive away scary images in future.

I asked him to teach Oscar the dog how to do this, just to be sure Oscar would never frighten himself with things he didn't understand. This 'teaching' process embedded Joel's new learning.

Expanding Joel's personal sense of pride was my chosen antidote to his feelings of not being trustworthy, and he seemed pleased to consider the possibility that the more he focused on this feeling, the more he would gain the trust of his parents.

Joel described his feelings of personal pride as a physical sensation that moved around his heart in a clockwise direction and was a bright orange colour. These were easy sensations to enhance through the Spinning Feelings technique we practised earlier.

Joel now needed some coaching in how to become more of the young man he wanted to be now that he was free from the 'infection'. We built lots of powerfully good feelings and glued them into his visualisations of seeing himself make smart decisions and notice how proud he felt.

My change work with Joel was soon over, as he could no longer find a way to scare himself or feel bad. He was ready to move on, but it was vital to set up a system that supported and reinforced the change. That meant some family coaching and a signpost to the work of Rosenthal and Jacobsen (the study which showed children achieved to the level of their teacher's expectations earlier in this chapter).

Using the power of language to direct his parents' attention I wrote some family coaching notes (opposite page).

JOEL'S FAMILY'S COACHING NOTES

*"**When** you reinstate parental controls ..."*
*"**Once** he has regained your trust..."*

o **Please act 'as if' it is all over** and allow him the space to move through this and grow new neural pathways rather than have him re-visit the old ones.

o **Avoid using words like 'self-control'**, which suggests there is something to *be controlled*, or something that could *get out of control*. Help him to feel his energy *flowing* and his mind moving *forwards towards* a rewarding future.

o **Focus his attention *towards* feeling proud** and growing up nicely or being more like Dad [his hero].

o Build self-esteem by helping him **find his own evidence** that he can make good decisions. Rather than offer adult judgement and opinion by saying things like '*well done*' or '*good lad*', simply ask him how he felt and direct his attention to his personal judgements that helped him feel good and make good decisions.

o Keep him **moving towards** feeling proud, open, and honest, etc. rather than have him moving away from feeling naughty, helpless, etc.

o **Trust him and help him to build trust in himself.**

Two years later, when I asked the family's permission to use this case study, Joel's mum said: *"Oh my, I had forgotten all about that horrible time..."*

Happy Brain™ Training Resilience Tip
The arts are synonymous with emotional expression, and I recommend everyone has some type of artistic, creative output for the sake of their emotional wellbeing, such as singing, dancing, drawing, painting, sculpting, acting, poetry or visualisation.

Activity: Demotion of emotion

Although we largely refer to the manifestations of the emotional brain as non-verbal communication, we can use language to get more specific and dilute the intensity of a feeling by talking 'about' it, i.e., the feeling (not the justification or perceived cause of the feeling).

Below are some words that can help you to explore emotions as a variety of descriptive words, rather than generalised ones like 'stress' or 'anxiety'. This exercise builds on 'Finding Feelings' in the last chapter. Easy words are *angry/sad/scared*, but their lack of specificity can hold you, and a child, stuck.

Each word will land in a unique way inside the neurological map. Try it for yourself. Say to yourself, '*I feel loved*', '*I feel cherished*', '*I feel appreciated*', '*I feel adored*'... Which words tug at the strongest emotion?

Now say to yourself, '*I feel hated, disgusting, awful, sad...*' again, notice the strength of emotion that is triggered by these words.

Your freedom (and that of any child) comes when you can use words to express your inner worlds and receive them as spoken truths of others. Practise using these and notice your responses.

AMUSED	HOPEFUL	ANXIOUS	FOOLISH
ACCEPTED	HUMOROUS	APPREHENSIVE	FRANTIC
CALM	LOVED	BITTER	GUILTY
CAPABLE	LOVING	BORED	HATEFUL
CHERISHED	PEACEFUL	DEFEATED	HORRIFIED
COMFORTABLE	PLAYFUL	DEJECTED	HOSTILE
CONFIDENT	QUIET	DEVASTATED	IGNORED
CONTENT	RELAXED	NEEDY	IMPATIENT
DELIGHTED	SAFE	DESPERATE	INDECISIVE
DESIRABLE	SATISFIED	DISAPPOINTED	INFERIOR
FORGIVING	CAREFREE	TRUSTING	INSECURE
FRIENDLY	CARELESS	EMBARRASSED	SECURE
SELF-RELIANT	PROTECTIVE	FEARLESS	ISOLATED
SILLY	INTUITIVE	MELANCHOLIC	JEALOUS
SUPPORTIVE	THOUGHTFUL	MUDDLED	TRAPPED
SYMPATHETIC	SENSITIVE	OLD	FREEDOM
GLAD	FORGIVEN	OUTRAGED	
GRATEFUL	INSENSITIVE	INDIGNANT	

Activity: Family charades

Most people know how to play charades or have their own version of it. Choose any variation. Stay clear about providing an opportunity for children to experiment with an ever-widening range of feelings; to do this they may want to pretend to be other people, characters, pop stars etc. Keep the space safe for the child by avoiding ridicule or judgement. Always end this (and any) game on a happy note, and if a child gets upset for any reason, keep the game going or add a distraction until everyone feels OK again. Remember, the Reptilian Brain has to feel *emotionally and physically safe* enough to 'expose' feelings. There should be no safer place than with you. *Our Happy Brain™ Coaching Kit mirrored emotions 'mirror the face' and are an easy alternative to charades, since all you have to do is take a lucky dip and mimic the emotion you have picked out. The more expressive and exaggerated, the better the mapping exercise.*

Do not label someone's emotional states

Instead, be curious about their evolving map and encourage them to express what is true for them.

Emotional expression with children is easy because we can do it through a range of actions, songs, dance, drawings, sculpture, metaphor, stories, etc. Adults tend to prefer to express themselves through language, yet often miss the opportunity to tune into this part of the brain's ability to be playful.

Note: Your assumption about someone's emotional state is precisely that – your *perception* and *judgements* based in your neurological map. Yet the smartest way to help someone to self-manage their feelings is to acknowledge whatever is their reality, before **leading them to a more resourceful emotional state.**

For example, *'You sound really sad about your cat being run over, shall we draw a picture of your sad feelings,* and then we can draw a picture of your happy memories of *Fluffy, and we can draw some really cute kittens after that...'*

If you deny someone else's experience (*'no, you're not scared'* or *'don't be sad ...'*) or ridicule it (*'that was ages ago'* or *'you're pathetic'*) you will set up confusion as to whose version of reality is to be trusted and is most valid. In turn, this builds patterns for conflict over who's reality is 'right' which, as we'll see, can cause personal and social dissonance.

Especially with children:

We do not want to teach patterns of inordinate trust in external *or* internal opinion. Instead we want to:

o   Trust their personal sensory experiences (even if we perceive them differently)

o   Ask questions to balance internal and external information

o   Welcome feedback to feed-forward

67

We are beginning to mark the differences between 'my map' and 'your map' and 'our map' and 'their map':
Thrive is based in *respecting* and *flowing* with someone else's map.
Survive is based in *defending* and/or *asserting* your own map. **Stress** is based in *mistrust*

Summary: The Mammalian Brain in Stress or Survival

When someone's emotional wellbeing is in a state of Stress or even Survive, you will see or hear:

o Limiting beliefs as generalisations about themselves and their world, e.g. *"I always get things wrong; people don't like me."*

o Belief-clinging e.g. must be right and cannot be wrong because their survival brain needs to predict feeling safe and secure.

o Expression of extreme (hyper and hypo) emotional responses with no mid-range or little flow between states.

o Poor boundaries for who/what triggers emotional reactions and inappropriate dependency on, or rejection of, others.

o Poor self-control when provoking emotional responses from others.

o Poor self-awareness and calibration (measurement) of self in relation to others.

o Inability to modify behaviours acceptable to the dominant social group.

Summary: The Mammalian Brain in Thrive

When someone's emotional wellbeing is in a state of Thrive, you will see or hear:

o Beliefs about themselves and their world that help them learn and focus on rewarding goals, e.g. *'of course I make mistakes; that's what helps me learn what to do differently next time.'*

o Belief-changing capabilities through a willingness to ask questions and entertain new ideas.

o Expression of a wide range of emotional responses in appropriate response to the environment.

o Strong boundaries for who/what triggers emotional responses with independence, co-operation and appropriate interdependence.

o Elicitation (getting) of purposeful and useful emotional responses from others.

o Self-awareness & calibration (measurement) of oneself in relation to others.

o Modification of behaviours in relation to the rules of the social group.

Summary: The Principle of Resilience

In this chapter, we have explored the Mammalian Brain's use of emotion to attract attention, detect threat and transmit survival information. Emotion is the glue that ensures vital information is memorable. The Mammalian Brain is the key communicator between 'upstairs' (the Thinking Mind) and 'downstairs' (the Reptilian Brain) as well as with the external world.

Balanced emotions **attract** useful and appropriate attention and **transmit** feelings of calm, trust and safety. Thrive emotions help to **motivate** success and access powerful states of mental rehearsal through visualisation. Emotional stability means being able to re-balance the brain, whenever and wherever we want. In the next chapters, we will connect to your Mammalian Brain's author, director and co-creator of happiness, the Thinking Mind.

BEFORE WE MOVE ON, PLEASE CAPTURE YOUR THOUGHTS:

» Questions   » Comments   » Insights

CHAPTER FOUR

"The Thinker can think virtually anything... the Prover is a much simpler mechanism. It operates on one law only: Whatever the Thinker thinks, the Prover proves"

ROBERT ANTON WILSON

AUTHOR, ESSAYIST, FUTURIST (1932-2007)

CHAPTER FOUR (a):
WHEN THE LIGHTS ARE ON, BUT NO ONE'S HOME

So far, we've explored Happy Brain™ as a model that helps us to understand how Survive / Thrive patterns are triggered and what we can do to influence them in ourselves, in others and especially in children. Now it's time to visit the prefrontal cortex, our seat of rational Thinking; the conductor of attention and the reins for conscious brain training. **With one very important exception...**

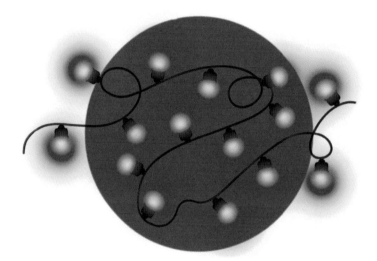

SURVIVE

If a Survival reaction is triggered, all energies are diverted from the top/front of our brain to support lightning-fast automatic Survival reactions in the lower (Mammalian and Reptilian) regions. The Thinking Mind is not necessary for survival energy and chemical encoding of memories.

Later, however, after the threat has passed and cognitive functions are back online, the Thinking Mind engages complex cognitive evaluations to make sense of what has just happened. New experience is compared with previously encoded memories to evaluate and conclude meaning, predict recurrence, and plan navigations for (any) next time. Creative juices then flow in the Thinking Mind and a 'story' emerges that helps self-soothe the Stress and make the 'story' easy to access.

Convincing one's social group that the story is valid feels reassuring and helps group survival. Emotions are key to communicating a story that will be memorable and provoke emotions in others. Words provoke emotions. **Storytelling is therefore a treasured survival strategy.**

70

CHAPTER FOUR (b):
THE PRINCIPLE OF CLARITY

In this chapter, we view the Thinking Mind (prefrontal cortex) as the conscious mind; rational, logical and capable of complex calculations that can organise peak physical, emotional and mental performance. To do this well and drive Thrive, the upper (Thinking) and lower (Reptilian and Mammalian) regions need to communicate coherently. Chaos can occur if there is conflict between 'top-down' and 'bottom-up' messages, limiting physical, emotional and mental performance potential. We might call this 'dissonance'.

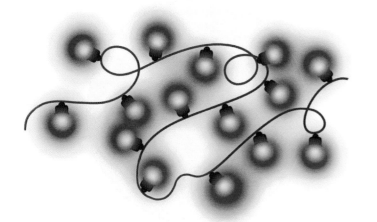

STRESS   THRIVE

Clarity is the ability to evaluate and direct your **attention on purpose,** to:

- o Physical sensations
- o Emotional responses
- o New and novel thoughts (imagination)
- o Old, habituated thoughts (memories)
- o Perceptions of time (past, present, future)
- o Thoughts that trigger Stress/Survive reactions
- o Thoughts that trigger Thrive responses (choice)
- o Sensory feedback feeding forward to decisions

- o Personal narratives that support or hinder goals
- o Social narratives that provide a greater sense of purpose
- o Awareness and respect of the perceptions of others
- o Verbal and non-verbal expressions
- o Decisions that lead to actions

THINKING

Apparently, we think an average of 70,000 thoughts a day, and it is said that most of those thoughts are just randomly firing neurological patterns on a (metaphoric) rinse and repeat, dependent on tried and trusted pathways, stimulated by ongoing fragments of sensory information. Thoughts that catch/need our attention are generally those with the highest emotional charge.

Daydreaming is an example of getting lost in pleasant thoughts energised by Thrive Brain states; this is fantastic for problem solving as all neural pathways are available to access, creatively combine, bridge and alchemise a new idea or discover a solution.

Meditation and hypnosis are easy ways to access this 'super-brain', where deep, whole-brain relaxation gives the Thinking Mind access to deeper states and superpowers. There is no sense of 'time' in a meditative or hypnotic state, simply access to rich inner resourcefulness as energies ebb and flow naturally.

Some people *believe* (remember, beliefs are just habits that we have unconsciously learned to value) their superpower is to think lots of thoughts energised by Stress states; generating overwhelm and building masses of 'reactional' energy.

Too much of this kind of *catastrophising*, without taking an 'action' to release the Stress, will debilitate the whole system, which in turn can trigger a Survival reaction. The Reptilian Brain needs to be given an action that discharges pent-up Survival energy.

In a highly Stressed state, the brain is reactive and makes poor decisions or fixates on a single thought that it can't resolve. Without resolving and discharging

about their respective tiredness and difficult workdays (as if it were a competition to see who worked hardest). Lo and behold, the toddler would react with a tantrum, which led to more arguments about who had the best parenting style.

They tried to negotiate with the toddler - *'speak to me, tell me what's wrong'* or *'what is it that you want?'* or *'you know you have to have a bath now'* or *'don't be a naughty girl'* or *'be a good girl'* - all of which either fell on deaf ears or aggravated the child further **because they were trying to meet the child in the wrong part of her brain.**

The parents' reasoning skills were in a state of dissonance, while the young child's (already limited by age) reasoning skills were now completely off-line. I explained that the time for using verbal language (aimed to the higher, Thinking Mind of the prefrontal cortex) came later, once they had led the child out of rage (lower brain) and settled into Thrive.

Settling the Reptilian Brain had to be their priority for their initial interaction; some tips included generating a rhythm by splashing or with bath toys, playing calming background music, singing familiar songs, humming, a gentle rhythmic body wash, soothing/stroking arms, back and forehead, speaking soft calm words (*'reeelaaax, it's ooookaaaay, looooooovely girl'*), using calm sounds (*'hmmmmn, ooooooooo, thaaaaaat's niiiiiiice'*) as gifts to their daughter's neurological map.

Of course, in being focused on creating calm states for the child, the parents themselves would have to be

Stress, energies can become erratic, trapped and toxic to wellbeing.

Think – Feel – Do is an easy algorithm to use for yourself and one that kids easily understand. We call this 'top-down' thinking where you use your Thinking Mind to drive Thrive. You can also use your Thinking Mind to drive 'bottom-up' Thrive by noticing which brain part is most out of kilter and deciding what to do to re-balance it.

When a client asked me for advice about her toddler who was having tantrums almost every bath time at the end of each day, she inadvertently conceded that she and her partner would regularly bicker in those states first. But this means they had to **decide** to teach their toddler to associate bath time with fun and relaxation and then take **action** to achieve it, ideally ahead of time.

Preparing themselves, their child and their environment would also help the flow of good feelings between each of them. A super-smart strategy would be to mentally rehearse positive bath time experiences during the day by play-acting fun, relaxing bath times with dolls or toy animals, or through drawing pictures of the desired outcome.

SPEAKING OF CONFLICT...

If someone – anyone - around you is in a Survival state (lower, Reptilian Brain), you will be wasting your time trying to use logic and language (the higher, Thinking Mind) to resolve any dispute. If they are in a highly stressed state, you may find your instinct to argue flares out of *nowhere* (it actually comes from your own primitive fight reaction).

In this case, **your smart-thinking Thrive choice is to attend to *stabilising your own state first.***

Any ongoing *temptation* to argue comes from your *thinking* about the situation, which jerks emotions that fuel Stress. Catch your judgements! In my trainings, I ask delegates to think of a critical thought/judgement about someone and to draw an icon that represents it (think – feel). I then provide clear plastic glasses and have them draw the icon over each lens. This helps them to see the 'filter' that obscures their Thrive.

This is another **think-feel-do** activity, which, if you decide to pursue it, will fill your body with Stress energy, so take care to discharge it later. In the meantime, it will leak out through your physical movements, facial expression and the tone of your voice.

74

Most people have been on the receiving end of a particularly vindictive undertone that masked the words being spoken. Most people have also discharged stress energy in this way too. Survival energy that gets discharged as an emotional force behind the spoken word is a mighty weapon, *detrimental* to the *wellbeing* of *both the speaker and the receiver.*

The opposite is also true; speaking through an emotion of compassion or loving kindness is also a powerful force behind the spoken word. It is a gift to the other person and for yourself - a Win-Win.

When you realise this, you have a choice:
- o *The Thrive choice* when receiving super stress-charged words *from another person,* is to allow the other person (or help them) to cool off and wait until their Thinking Mind is back online before attempting a conciliation. Or walk away.
- o *The Thrive choice* if you find yourself receiving super stress-charged words *from your internal voice (self-talk),* is also to allow yourself to re-balance and respond only when your Thinking Mind is back online.

Fight or flight words, sounds or imaginations can be terrifying to everyone involved. Ideally, we want to head them off. Or let them pass. They are simply survival messages from the lower brain. Attend to that first.

When you can stay conscious of what you're saying, a rational mind can help to build your future capacity for flourishing.

That includes becoming aware of, and harnessing, the stories you might build to excuse, justify, defend or condemn certain behaviours.

Now let's explore some of the ways we use storytelling...

Personal narrative is a story that the conscious mind makes up to try to make rational sense of life experience:

o   *"I'm a good girl"* may be a statement of **congruence** because my thoughts and feelings match **evidence from my neurological map.**

o   *"I'm a good girl"* may be a statement of **incongruence** if my conscious mind is trying to believe the statement, with little or **no evidence from my neurological map** yet.

The personal narrative is how we build and reveal our sense of who we think we are; our **identity**. It is still a story, however; one that continually evolves through life and has many authors, keen to tell us who they think we are.

We trade personal narratives with each other to enhance our social positioning and convince others of our value. We can secure attention from others through our narratives and direct the attention of others through our anecdotes or gossip.

We'll further explore the motivations for storytelling later. For now, Happy Brain™ encourages people to do three things with narratives:

o   *Observe* them with a hefty dose of objectivity

o   *Build* powerful narratives that propel Thrive motivations

o   *Let go* of narratives that generate stress energy

Letting go of the need to engage in a harmful narrative switches our brains to Thrive. On the other hand, *defending or justifying* poor behaviour by constructing an excuse for it will contribute to more patterns of stress.

Social narrative is a story that defines the social group. We value belonging to a social group (family, gang, school, club, team, business, religion, town, country, etc) and it is therefore natural that we should want to protect and defend it, unless we choose to switch allegiance to a new group that fits us better (teenagers do this best).

Most social groups have some sort of figurehead or 'leader' who maintains a social order to support Thrive. A group that is dissonant can easily become emotionally unstable with irrational Survival-like behaviours and a me/you – them/us mindset that tries to second-guess the next threat.

Thrive-based groups **share stories of success and co-operation and celebrate stories of collaboration that recognise a 'we' pattern.**

Social media encourages us to 'trade' our personal narratives and expose our perceived social value by declaring who we know or are connected to, what we look like, and how we behave. Psychology calls this *social positioning.*

This is a very tough call for teenagers who, in needing to conform to the social norm, are encouraged to get validation from the outside world and mostly from complete strangers. To the Mammalian Brain, the results of this can be glorious (social adoration) or terrifying (rejection). Or worse still – invalidation.

These feelings are probably non-negotiable, but we

can help teenagers **'think about'** and understand the bigger picture and understand the social structures that manipulate their emotional brains.

We can help them make more informed decisions about whether or not to play the game. I find Happy Brain™ is a great model to help teenagers to identify for themselves which brain parts are involved in their behaviours.

I remember chatting to a teenager who was addicted to online gaming. We explored his Reptilian Brain rewards, his Mammalian Brain rewards, and then researched and rationalised (using the Thinking Mind) the structures of the gaming industry. His beliefs shifted from *'they're good guys wanting to provide us with fun games'* to *'they're rich guys who need us to be addicted so they can get richer'.*

It's never my job to indoctrinate, but by leading thoughts to see what else is possible does seem a responsible and important job.

YOUNG MUMS

I remember having coffee with another mum who was relatively new to the school gate. As I left her house a few hours later, I felt drained, exhausted and disinclined to repeat the experience ever again.

She had systematically talked about every person we jointly knew in a bid to get my opinion. I guess it was a bonding exercise, except her filters were fixated on what she *didn't like* about other people. I felt contaminated by her intense emotional reactions and now realise the toxicity came from her fears, Stress and probably even Survival needs. Interestingly, her daughter was quite a (verbal) bully at school. No wonder really, the poor girl probably didn't know how else to 'discharge' her toxic feelings and had therefore imprinted the language patterns of her parent.

Scripts are auto-pilot stories that are easily accessed, carry little substance but have a social currency. Saying 'sorry' is the simplest example I can think of. It trips off the tongue and is deemed socially desirable. Yet when you feel the energy behind the word as empty and meaningless, it sets up mistrust. We have a family joke about one of our kids who used to say *'soh-reyy'* in an offended tone. More than once, I've been accused of 'not saying sorry' and my answer is always the same: if I say it, I mean it and you will feel it. For me this is integrity.

We trade our personal narratives as a way to get attention (Survival) or to contribute wisdom to the wellbeing of the group (Thrive). It's worth considering which narratives you use to help yourself Thrive and help others also. And which narratives get you attention, and from whom. Many parents 'trade' stories about their children's successes and failures while others 'trade' stories about their personal lives.

One of my failures as a mind coach involved a young family which seemed entirely invested in having a child riddled with (medical mystery) illnesses, irrational fears and a plethora of phobias. The adolescent was finally being home-schooled and had withdrawn from everything and everyone except her parents. Naturally, they were concerned and verbalised their heated disappointment of 'being let down' by doctors, nurses, schools, psychologists, psychiatrists, social workers, therapists and more.

I was naïve to believe they wanted freedom for their child, because mystery illnesses, fears and phobias are generally quite simple interventions. The bit I missed was that I was being invited to validate their narrative, about which they were verbose, and the child remained silent, except for reassuring glances to the parents whenever I asked as question to which the reply was '*I don't know*'. I eventually asked the parents to leave the room (unusual in my work, since I always work with the whole system/family) and softly unfolded an adolescent who was absolutely stymied by the parents' needs. Within 20 minutes, a light within the child stared to glow as we played and chatted about apparently benign things so I got to see/hear/feel how she could build new patterns for Thrive. All light faded as soon as the parents came back into the room, where I failed to convince them of their child's 'potential', triggering a double-headed defensive reaction.

That was a salutary lesson in the importance of staying in rapport with the whole system and all parts within. Next time, I would know to work within the parents' map of reality first, in order to lead them to see what they hadn't yet been able to perceive.

Another lesson for me about social narratives came from a 10-year-old child who was apparently 'suicidal'. I deal with lots of suicidal people of all ages and this child didn't fit the usual pattern. Instead, I sensed 'a script' rather than the emotional states and stories of someone wanting to end their life. I suspected that they had succumbed to a trend about teenage suicide, and indirectly this turned out to be true.

A mental health charity had visited the school to talk about suicide in children as part of a national awareness campaign. During the talk, the child had wandered into imaginations of '*how would I kill myself?*' building a number of pictures and sounds (thoughts) eventually settling on imagining hanging to death. Terrifying - **and a brain that is scared will try to make sense of the feeling.**

This child concluded they 'must be suicidal' since they were having 'thoughts' about suicide, just like the charity said could happen, and therefore followed the charity's advice and told a teacher. A ton of social/psychological and psychiatric intervention later, the smart parents brought the child to me. A few mind magic hypnosis repatterns later and the child was free from the terrors (scary pictures that triggered scary feelings) of suicidal thoughts and armed with new 'mind magic' skills to deal with other intrusive thoughts.

However, the child was now on the radar of a well-intentioned but ill-informed system that regularly prompted '*are you ok, are you still suicidal...?*'

Just before reaching adolescence, the prefrontal cortex (Thinking Mind) suddenly grows new pathways, and in so doing increases the potential for imagination. I remember (as a 10-year-old) having some dental surgery which required a light anaesthetic. The dental surgeon said to me, '*you need to go to the bathroom before we begin*'. I went to the bathroom and waited, and waited, too afraid to pee in case I missed the very important thing (in my imagination) that was supposed to happen – in the bathroom, having taken the instruction, literally.

Entering into the imaginations of a young child is key to helping them move through and find new answers, rather than getting stuck.

TEENAGE NARRATIVES

Teenage years are often a stressful time of raging hormones and rapid bodily changes coinciding with serious decisions about which new social group to bond with. And to make matters even more tricky, the teenage prefrontal cortex (Thinking Mind) actually shrinks (it goes through a period of natural pruning), which means the executive functioning skills of risk evaluation and impulse control, are less accessible.

This period lasts until the early twenties, by which

77

time many unhealthy patterns may have become ingrained. This perfect storm needs to be navigated with care and guided towards Thrive to make the best (possible) evaluation of options, because:

o Stress brains default to the scripts of their surrounding groups.

o Survival brains choose safety first, which may involve complying with the values of a wayward social group or gang or fighting to control the home.

Teenage years can be tricky for both teenagers and parents, as teenagers need to explore new territories beyond family 'narratives' and experiment with aspects of their new social groups, which may not fit the map of their nest. Established rules and parameters may no longer make sense. This often feels exhilarating (and frightening) to the teenager and challenging to the parents. Many kids suddenly shift from being exemplary to engaging a parent's worst fears.

Teenage warfare is a common theme in my work, as parents realise that 'their' script for their child no longer matches the child's narrative. I get a lot of well-meaning parents telling me all about their child with great pride or great disdain. Perhaps this will be the topic of my next book!

Whose map is it anyway?
"What do you want?" I asked the dad.
"To enjoy what I do again – better work/life balance," he replied sincerely.
"Tell me more?" I enquired ambiguously, to gather more information.
"Well I mean, I'd like to spend more time as a family, with the children," he said, nodding to himself.
"More time? One or two minutes a week?" I teased.

"Oh no ... oh ... um... probably 20 minutes more - each day," he concluded. *"20 minutes a day - watching TV?"* I quizzed with a twinkling eye.
"No, I mean spending 20 minutes a day with Jo and his homework," he reasoned.
I invited him to consider *"What will that do for you?"*
"Well then Jo will get better grades," he asserted.
"And..." I paused
"I want him to achieve more," he insisted.
"And what does Jo want?" I chided.
And the penny dropped ...

Remember, the essence of this book is to build a **prevention model,** and to do this, we need to be clear about the ways that we, as adults, can easily contribute to the uncertainties of growing up. The following notes were sent to me by a kind, loving father of a 15-year-old lad who was seeking help. I've highlighted key phrases in bold that we can learn from:

Pete has always been an outgoing and expressive child growing up, so it's been quite a noticeable change since he's hit the teenage years how introverted he's become.

He's our oldest, so we're figuring this out as we go... was it just 'a phase'? **He said he did a personality test – maybe a year ago? – and was 'an introvert' and I think he has become more-so since.** *I thought it was his 'coping mechanism' for school life; he doesn't like conflict, and so my thinking is he's become 'invisible' – his word – to avoid trouble. He also told me last week that he's anxious about getting a teacher's question wrong, about "going red", so he doesn't say anything in class.*

That's consistent with the fact that every teacher we spoke to at his school Options Evening in January said he needed to contribute more in class. In the past, he's told us most people outside his close friendship group think he's quiet and a loner, but that's not been the case in the

78

past and it's not the case with his friends. Recently, Pete revealed to his mum that he thought he was 'depressed' and needed help. In discussion, he talked about how he felt he couldn't express happiness (like his sister could) or his frustrations.

Whilst he expressed that 'it took me long enough' to say something, we reassured him that it was great that he'd said something at all.

I talked to him that evening and he mentioned the pressure at school, and particularly the pressure he puts on himself – comparing himself/his performance to others. I got the impression that whilst his strategy has been to be 'low profile' to avoid bother at school, it's gone too far, and he's become 'invisible'.

Pete said to me what he wants are tools and techniques to help him be more expressive. He's said he's nervous about a session with you, 'because you know what I'm like speaking to people I don't know', but he recognises he's still after help, and that's part of the process.

What an intuitive dad! Working with Pete to help him express himself and build Happy Brain™ Thrive tools was easy because the *whole system* (in this case, family) was invested in building patterns of Thrive.

This anecdote perfectly sums up many, many 'teenage' troubles, worries and difficulties, which left unmanaged can easily spiral into serious mental and emotional health issues. We really must learn from the kids!

This example does make me wonder about easy access to psychological profiling without expert guidance to counter the generalisation, i.e. *'you are an introvert'*. That sounds like a command rather than a useful script or narrative. How did that 'box' close down the lad's options? How did he interpret it? What were the thoughts and feelings that tilted him

to become 'too introvert' and then explore situations where he felt more balanced? Did the profiling exercise teach him how to adjust his thoughts and feelings to cope with different situations, or to adjust the story he was telling himself? No. He said no. My job was to boost his self-confidence in being true to himself with skills to re-balance as needed.

LISTENING

It's often said that we listen *to find our moment to speak*, rather than *to hear what is being said*. We certainly decide what to listen *for* and the Thinking Mind does a mighty fine job of filtering incoming sensory data to meet our personal narrative of how things are. The 'decision' about what to listen for may be unconscious or conscious; brain training helps you focus your filters.

While your whole nervous system acts as an instrument of receiving and transmitting information, processing billions of bits of sensory data every second, it also learns to prioritise which sensory channel to pay most attention to. Remember the plastic specs that filter through judgements?

Hearing is the first sense to develop in utero, so it's a reasonable assumption that it may be more valuable to our survival.

o **Stressed brains** scan the environment for any semblance of threat, and hearing is an important radar with specific fragments of sound prioritised as key data. This creates an interference pattern in the way we can listen.

o **Thrive brains,** on the other hand, are receptive to a wide range of sensory stimuli and we can more freely 'decide' what to listen for.

Many brains, especially in young and vulnerable people, may listen to language **literally**. A small child overhearing a hungover parent saying *'I feel like I'm* *dying'* may become vigilant and run a Stress brain. Similarly, overhearing a parent say *'he really is a terrible child'* doesn't give the child's brain much processing potential. It's a statement of fact.

What should the child do now? What pictures and sounds might the child be making inside their mind's eye and ear, triggered by sloppy generalisations?

If you tell your child as they leave for school, *'I'm sad to be alone all day'* or *'I'm going to be really angry if you don't do well in your test'*, this could set up their filters for feeling responsible for your wellbeing. **That seems an unfair responsibility** for the child, who could end up with feelings of overwhelm from trying to please everyone else.

Building self-awareness is key to wellbeing because Thinking Mind is always adjusting itself according to its own records of existence and will always seek to prove its own theory about the world.

Self-awareness is the best tool to **modify** thoughts, feelings and behaviours that build more rewarding relationships. For instance, *"I get angry when my child misbehaves'* probably means *'because it makes me look like a bad parent';* indeed a stressful thought that could turn to anger.

It might also reveal an underlying tension between the personal narrative of *'I'm a good parent'* and belief of *'I'm not a good enough parent'*.

Once this pattern is made conscious, all sorts of possibilities can unfold to everyone's benefit, e.g. *'I'm doing my best as a parent; sometimes I get angry when my child doesn't do as I want, so I'm learning new ways communicate with him'.*
Self-awareness builds congruence!

Get your own clarity!
I have found a really useful thought is the **self-inquiry:** *'who is this about?'* Or, *'what's the purpose of what I'm about to say/do?'*

Listening for meaning
o Certain words hold strong emotional charges; stressful, calming, exciting etc.
o Certain sounds trigger high stress or instant calm.
o Certain combinations of words and sounds trigger a cascade of images.
o Certain visual stimuli will spark imaginations as we **try to make meaning.**

Understanding these patterns helps us to listen and explore meaning rather than reacting to an **assumption** about what we think.

We have a tendency to gather more of the same kind of information – good or bad. If you perceive the world to be benevolent, you will seek sensory confirmation of this. The opposite is also true. These are patterns, not truths.

Many suicidal people cannot see beyond these filters; inadvertent brain training by life's whirlwinds and other people's narratives can extinguish all hope. People get trapped in their neurological patterns and don't know a way out. So they opt out.

What can we learn from children about 'thinking traps?'
An exercise I regularly use with children to help them identify their thinking traps is one where they start off by identifying:
o I see... and it makes me feel... (using the PES)
o I hear... and it makes me feel... (using the PES)

Then, once we've established the 'direct' see-hear-feel association, I ask them to add in another layer: **because I think it means …**

This activity quickly reveals how 'interpretations' of sensory-based information can cause great distress and often expose underpinning beliefs. Once we've gathered this information, I then teach them how to 'undo thinking traps' with a simple formula which we will look at later.

First of all, let's look at the kind of things that commonly trigger stress in children through their own work from my Happy Brain™ sessions.

Gathering this kind of information helps us to understand how patterns of Stress are developing in young minds based on their **interpretation** of sensory information.

If only kids could learn to use their smart Thinking Mind to better evaluate what they see/hear, they would be more able to switch off unnecessary stress.

This is a vital skill for children, yet most adults are unaware of the 'seemingly trivial' things children worry about that can snowball into making life-limiting decisions.

This helps us to understand barriers to learning

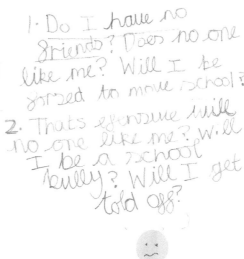

I see – I hear – I think unhappy

1 • I see my friends running away from me.

• Something happens and eve

4 • I see my favourite top which has shrunk in the wash

2 • I hear my friends saying mean things about me how

• My friend I hear my friend 3 telling everyone that something which I don't do

1 • I think that they don't want to be my friends.

2 • I think that I have horrible hair

3 • I think that they are trying to get me in trouble.

4 • People should look after my things

I see – I hear – I think unhappy

Of course, we could simply 'tell' children not to worry about the things they write, and 'assure' them that their reality is not at all accurate. After all, adults know best, don't they?

Or instead we can put aside our own mental maps and lead children to discover something new about themselves. The latter leads their own experience into new brain patterns which support new possibilities for problem solving. *This is the key to self-esteem...*

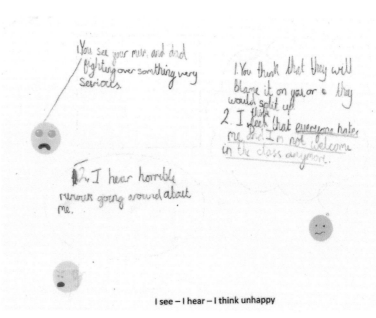

1. You see your mum and dad fighting over something very serious.

2. I hear horrible rumours going around about me.

1. You think that they will blame it on you or e they would split up

2. I feel that everyone hates me and I'm not welcome in the class anymore.

I see – I hear – I think unhappy

Undo thinking traps

My favourite *'undo thinking traps'* game in a classroom or social group is to separate the group into As and Bs who line up facing each other.

As = **buddies** who face the PowerPoint screen.

Bs = have with them their sheets of **see/hear > feel > because I think it means ...**

For 1 minute:

Bs tell As what they have assumed to be true (reading from their sheets)

Buddies respond with the following questions (read off the PowerPoint screen):

What's the worst thing that thought could mean?

What's the best that thought could mean?

What's the most likely thing it could mean?

What else could it mean?

What would someone else think it could mean?

Bs answer each question until the first minute is signalled.

Then Bs move one place along to their left and begin the process all over again for another minute.

The process repeats several times until Bs have exhausted all possible answers (thus *self-diluting their beliefs*) while As have now learned a buddy 'script' that they can use again at home, in the playground etc.

Now roles reverse and the activity repeats.

This activity is one of the children's favourite Happy Brain™ games and I use it with adults too. I believe it builds capacity to support each other in future and it introduces the importance of asking smart questions and finding new answers. By having someone help you to change meaning, the emotion is reduced, which in turn settles the lower brain. This is 'top-down' smartness. And you can do it for yourself.

This introduces you to the **linguistic** part of Neuro Linguistic Programming. Within the NLP framework, the Meta Model provides an extremely powerful tool to **conversationally change brain states** through targeted questions; our child's play model introduces you to the ease of shifting someone's 'limiting' perspective through well-targeted questions.

Look at the first example of see-hear-think-unhappy (previous page) where the child writes:

o "do I have no friends?"

o "does no-one like me?"

o "will I be forced to leave school?"

First of all, note that they are asking themselves these questions based on an assumption they are making. **They are presupposing something is true** (presuppositions are a powerful hypnotic technique) e.g. *it's possible to have 'no friends' and be 'forced to leave school'.*

Since their brain cannot possibly answer those questions accurately, they put themselves in a bind by searching for an answer through the same filter that is causing the problem. Their belief is simple hypnosis in action. Asking your brain a question that is impossible to answer is one of the most common stress patterns I find in clients of all ages. What's the purpose of asking yourself a question like this? To confirm or predict the worst? And then what will you do with the answer? What does it tell your brain to do next? Nothing! **It's a trap!**

Generally, adults will answer these statements from a child with something like, *'of course you do! Don't be silly! You're such a stress-head!'* Because adults generally value their own opinions highly and assert their mental map as the one true reality, or seize their opportunity to provide a rescue service.

Adults feel good by doing this, but it **doesn't shift the child's stress feeling or tell their brain 'how' to**

83

figure a way out of the feeling, or what to do next.
Leaving a brain in a dissonant state, unable to relax, is a barrier to learning. Please avoid doing this!

A gift that builds resilience and self-esteem is **adults helping children undo thinking traps.** A Happy Brain™ coach might ask *'what did you see or hear that gave you that thought?... a sad face?... let's think of five reasons why that person might have a sad face':*

o They have a tummy ache
o They are worried about their pet
o They think no-one likes them (!)
o They are worried about missing their favourite TV programme
o They have just farted and now they're embarrassed

The possible perspectives are endless – the point is, we want to lead their mind to other 'possible' meanings. Suggesting 3) *'they (the sad-faced person) thinks no-one likes them'* forces the child into considering the other person's experience through the same filter that is causing them distress.

The final (farting) suggestion is unexpected, unpredictable and takes their brain down a whole new set of neurological pathways, instantly prompting laughter which produces a sudden influx of great **Thrive** brain chemistry to dilute the **Stress** brain chemistry. It **interrupts the pattern** they were stuck in. Their brain has to go somewhere new and break a habitual reaction. So, we can 'dilute' meaning and 'interrupt' habitual thinking, just by asking a few questions. Now we have to help their brains move forward towards more rewarding behaviours.

Evaluation notes: Happy Brain™ Assistant during Year 3 workshop

When I see/hear...I think...I feel... exercise: The kids seemed able to come up with problems, although some had trouble at first classifying the problem as something heard or seen, as they were thinking of the problem as a whole. Most of the kids mixed up thoughts and feelings. An example of the kind of thing I saw is "I feel why did she do that?" In cases like this, when I discussed it with them, they were then able to break the parts down into a thought and a feeling. I think that of the work I saw, only one girl followed the instructions to the letter, and only wrote down the thoughts. To the other kids, it seemed a bit of a surprise to them that what they had written down as "thoughts" were actually about their "feelings". Many kids wanted to write lots of example problems.

Some told me that their examples weren't real, just constructed examples, and yet they were able to associate with the examples and think about what they would think and feel in such a situation.

When we moved on to the questions about the problems (what's the best/worst/most likely etc.), some of the kids had difficulty understanding what was meant by the question "what else could it mean?" In most of these cases, however, their partner or someone else in the class could provide an example answer, which prompted their own thinking and answers.

I noticed that a lot of the boys wrote in their (day) evaluations that they liked this part a lot and enjoyed asking questions about other people's problems.

They also, of course, liked the fact that this was done standing up as a role play and magic wands were used.

BRAIN AIM

Unless we aim our brains *towards* something worthwhile and recognisable, we will default to old familiar patterns of thought, feelings and behaviour. It's the easy option, but don't be surprised when you can't get new results. Re-setting a brain aim requires a decision, which is easier than you think. You can do this for yourself to experience what we call in NLP well-formed outcomes. This principle is fundamental is to wellbeing because it takes the 'whole brain' into consideration. For our desired outcomes to be 'well-formed', we need to consider the following:

i. Positive language

We need to give the brain a **precise** thing to focus on, unlike in the example *'because I think it means I have no friends; no-one likes me, and will I be forced to leave school'*. There is nothing for the executive control centre to process here and so it simply extracts meaning from the emotional content alone.

People often need a hand to find out what they want, and an easy way to do this is to play 'opposites'. For example, *'what's the opposite of no-one liking you/ having no friends/being forced to leave school?'* The answer should give you something of value to discuss until you can establish **what they precisely want.**

Do you remember the happy-sad senses case study in Chapter 3, where the child wrote *'no sweeties, no Christmas presents, no money'*? This is a common example of inefficient thinking, using too much brain energy imagining something for the future and then 'virtually' removing it. Chaotic potential indeed!

ii. Under your sphere of control

'I want lots of friends and everyone liking me', might be a common goal stated in the positive, but it isn't within the child's control to achieve this because we cannot control the actions of other people. Negotiating this brain aim activity with a child can take some time, until they define what they *can* control (thoughts, feelings, behaviours) and we might then re-visit the goal, stated in the positive, as *'I want to feel confident and happy at school so that I can be a good friend to others'*. Is this within their control? Yes.

iii. Reality-based

Is *'I want to feel confident and happy at school so I can be a good friend to others'* possible in the real world? Yes. If *'I want people to like me'* pops up, take them back to the first stage of goal setting that is within their sphere of control, i.e. *'I want to feel likeable'*.

iv. Sensory-imprinted

We've looked at the importance of mental rehearsal which helps builds a new programme for automatic pilot. The fastest way to do this is to talk them through the sensory experience 'as if' the goal was already achieved', as follows: **'When** *you feel confident and happy and likeable, what will you see, feel, hear, (smell/ taste), do? What will others see/hear/feel?'* Engaging the full sensory experience of visualisation helps them create and step into their own hero movie, where they imprint **new behaviours** in their neurological map. Now elicit some super great emotions associated to a phrase like 'super-you' and you have a direct link to that great memory for the future.

v. Ecology

What will they gain by achieving this goal? What will they lose by achieving this goal? Is there any reason they should not proceed? Will anyone be harmed if they proceed? Usually with children, the ecology check has little impact, but I've seen adults in meltdown when they realise the goal they thought they wanted is ill-formed and an impossible task for their brain to deliver.

Case Study: "I need to revise or I'm going to fail"

Charlie was a bright 16-year-old approaching GCSE exams. She was stressed, struggling and now quite miserable. She obsessed about revision, yet her brain couldn't run efficiently. Her narrative was "I need to revise or I'm going to fail". These are the notes I sent her after a coaching session...

Hi Charlie,

As promised, here is the summary of the work we did today. We chatted about:

o Over-thinking about your exams
o Using fear of failure as a motivation
o Feeling anxious/nervous after thoughts of failure stimulated stress response
o Stealing your energy away from having fun and feeling calm

We looked at the way anxiety/Stress triggers come from these main sources:

o **Real** threat that your *senses perceive* - you *see, hear, feel, smell or taste* something that could threaten your survival, e.g. a pan of oil is catching fire. In this case, your instant and intense Stress response will ensure your Survival and so it's useful and temporary.

o **Real** threat coming from *body signals* – a virus, bacteria, dehydration, malnourishment, toxins, sugar, hormones etc., that puts your mind and body under appropriate Stress as it tries to re-balance.

o **Imagined** threat – if you *imagine* failing an exam you'll worry and build feelings of stress, but since the stress has nowhere useful to go, it stays *trapped inside the nervous system*. If you keep adding to it, the Thinking Mind tries to make sense of the feeling and comes up with narratives like, *'there's something wrong with me, or it's his/her fault.'*

Eventually, a thinking habit forms and that doesn't help you move forward; it just tells you what feelings to avoid. Too many of these *'avoidance'* feelings gets you stuck.

If you hear yourself justifying the stress by saying things like, *'it's because'*, or *'that means'*, you know you have to take control of your attention and direct it towards a rewarding future. This is solution-focused thinking.

The **mind chatter/narrative** is key for you, and your mental, emotional and behavioural freedom/happiness will flourish more when you learn to challenge your own thinking traps and become solution-focused, e.g.

Thought: *'I need to revise or I'm going to fail'*

o Possible challenge: *'Is it really true that revision = success?'*
o Possible challenge: *'Is it more important to study longer – or study smarter?'*
o Possible challenge: *'How does my recall work best – calm and confident/stressed and worried?'*

It's good that you found it funny to have laughed at taking these thoughts so seriously. **Laughter releases oxytocin** – a feel good neuro-chemical! And smile! **Smiling releases serotonin** – the happiness molecule.

Metaphor: Life is like a game of chess! When you are the queen on a chess board you get to be creative, flexible and always find a way to move around the game. A thriving human could be considered majestic. Many humans take the role of a pawn; always making the same moves with limited results. Be like the queen! **Here are some cool brain hacks for you:**

Happy Brain™ hack#1
Change brain chemistry by deciding to take a daily dose of laughter, singing, humming and smiling to re-set your nervous system to **calm** instead of fear.

Happy Brain™ hack#2
Questions are power arrows to direct your imagination.
Statements/labels/judgements (narratives) on the other hand, hold you stuck.
An example of this is you getting mad at your teacher and thinking *'Mrs B shouldn't have said x, y or z'* which holds you stuck in an emotional response that adds to your stress.
- o Power question alternative: *'what do I think she means?'*
- o Power question alternative: *'what else could it mean?'*
- o Power question alternative: *'is it possible she is trying to help me understand something important?'*
- o Power question alternative: *'what can I learn about myself from this feeling?'*

Applying a single meaning to what someone says limits everyone's personal freedom.

The trouble with Stress:
Thinking traps (applying a single meaning to words heard) stimulate feelings of Stress. The Basic Brain hears the alarm call and responds with an appropriate Stress response by switching on a power surge of:
- o Stress chemicals and hormones
- o Emergency supplies of fats and sugars
- o Faster breathing to increase oxygen levels
- o Increased temperature to prime muscles
- o Faster heartbeat to pump energy supplies

Then the nervous system becomes primed to Survive by fight or flight, and this instant power surge gives you a vital oomph to shift your body into a super-high performing gear to deal with any emergency situation

That response is useful if you have to suddenly run for the train or away from a wild animal, <u>but it's totally useless – and trapped - when you are lying in bed!</u>

Any Stress that lasts longer than a few minutes is being kept in an active state through over-thinking (*'it's because...' 'it means...'*)

Happy Brain™ hack#3
Aim your brain towards a rewarding future with brain-friendly language.
- » **Tell your brain what you want** *e.g. 'I want to feel calm and confident'.* This is a simple and precise aim, so your brain knows where to aim (remember the brain finds it hard to process a negative command such as 'I don't want to be Stressed' – stay clear with what you do want).
- » **Ask yourself if what you want is entirely within your control** - then you can go for it. If the goal involves someone else (e.g. *'I want*

him/her to change their opinion of me') your chances of success are limited and the price you pay (energy) is too high.

» **Do you have the resources you need?** Maybe that involves time to practice, money, books, videos, people, etc. Perhaps you already have the resources to practise calmness and clarity. Your intention is key.

» **Can you imagine the successful outcome?** Using all your senses, imagine looking, sounding, feeling calm, making healthy choices about study and practising success. *Super-charging* the pictures and sounds inside your mind is the breakfast of champions as it helps your brain clearly know its target. Even glimpses of these pictures and sounds are a starting point. Whatever you practise, you will habituate. Stay tenacious so the future Charlie thanks you for what you do today!

As we've said before, trying to get people to change their opinions or behaviour will deplete your reserves of available energy.

» **Useful mantra** (soft voice): *'Everything is just fine. I trust that my body and mind know how to take best care of me.'*

» **Useful imagery**: Push any scary mind's eye picture further away.

» **Useful feelings**: Relaxation.

> By managing her state and internal dialogue, Charlie went on to achieve outstanding grades.

Gathering information

What's the purpose of us gathering information and asking questions?

Some common reasons include:

o **Curiosity about other people's experiences:** We learn from other people's stories by making interpretive pictures and sounds inside our mind's eye/ear that create new pathways for us to access later.

o **Feelings of sharing someone's experience:** We feel connected when sharing an experience; feeling similar (and safe) with others builds rapport.

o **Proving your hypothesis:** We get a temporary feel-good when proving ourselves 'right'.

o **Looking for a rescue opportunity:** We feel secure when our mental map provides a solution for someone else, and we feel connected when it is accepted.

o **Working within the other person's map:** We can help people best when we stay out of our own opinions and assumptions and simply gather information from within the map that is creating the problem.
That's where answers will also be found. When we (metaphorically) drive alongside the other person, we might be able to guide them to new routes, paths, bridges and roadblocks. The calmer and more relaxed a person is, the more their own internal landscape potential will reveal itself.

A note about making assumptions

Assumptions help us predict. Making assumptions about others may be useful, but requires clarification.

An assumption that your friend's sad face means you have done something wrong is like reading their mind, only none of us can read minds - even though many people think they can!

We need to avoid looking inwardly to find answers that someone else needs to find for themselves. We can clarify any assumption we've formed by asking a question like, *'are you upset about something?'* which might open up a new dialogue.

Children learn their assumptions from adult narratives, and I often hear adult terms spewing from young mouths, getting etched in their expanding vocabulary and settling into belief streams. Kids as young as 8 say things like, *'he always needs to be right ...' 'she never smiles ...'*

What if you could?

The 'miracle question' is a coaching favourite where you ask someone *'if a miracle happened tonight while you sleep and tomorrow your problem had disappeared, what would it be like for you?'*

Just entertaining the idea in your imagination is a wonderful starting place to build the neurological pathways that might support you. My favourite way to do this is to say *'I'm not going to ask you to (change), but if you were the best possible version of you, what would you look, sound, feel like? Let's build a hologram of the person you would like to be, even though you don't yet think it's possible.'*

And then, when they're engaged through all their sensory imaginations*, I have them step into the skin of that holographic imagination, just to try it. Nothing is forced, but the pathways are primed, and motivation is more likely to come from within.

I always want to avoid:

o   Instruction to change that could be perceived defensively by the Reptilian Brain and set up conflict and reactionary behaviours.

o   Instruction to change that could set up dependency on the change worker.

In my work I strongly aim for independent thinking, and if an action is taken, the rewards all come from inside; building self-esteem.

*There are special language patterns in NLP called Representational Systems, that help us to engage the sensory channels more directly, and a special model of hypnosis called Milton Model, that helps to lead someone to explore inside their imagination.

89

A problem is a chance for you to do your best

DUKE ELLINGTON
COMPOSER AND JAZZ MUSICIAN

Case Study: NLP first aid

As first mum to hospital following a car crash involving my son and his two mates, I was able to quickly assess that (despite lots of blood and bruising) my son was OK. However, it was apparent that one of the other boys (Chris) was in quite a bad way.

After some time of full medical team attention, Chris was about to be left alone for a while, stabilised and in a semi-conscious state. At that time, his relatives were unaware of his situation, and I asked permission to go into his cubicle with to retrieve his mobile phone to call his family. Chris was semi-conscious, beyond scared and very distressed, trying desperately to make sense of the situations and fragments of things he had heard, felt and seen regarding his injuries.

Chris had long been a regular guest in our home, I knew him well and I quickly had to realise my immediate choices:

o I could stay focused on the task of retrieving the phone and leave him to his mind's distortions of what was happening to him and what he had overheard the medics discussing.
o I could become emotionally involved in my own drama of the experience.
o I could dissociate enough to utilise the skill set that I know could help him.

I chose the latter.

As is so often the way when we operate through unconscious competence within the other person's map of the world, it's hard to recall specifics, but I can share some NLP first aid points that noticeably improved Chris's state:

o **Neuro** - generating my own strong internal state of calm, confident energy re-assured his unconscious mind.
o **Linguistic** - utilising simple hypnotic language patterns (when you, as you …) I entirely presupposed his full recovery.
o **Programming** - quickly ascertaining how he was stressing himself in order to swiftly interrupt those patterns, re-frame his panic and re-direct his attention.

Words are powerful, and the way that each sound wave lands on your neurology shifts your experience. It is not rocket science. For example, if you say 'this' pain or 'that' pain, which feels more real and close up? Consider the differing impacts of these commonly heard questions:

o "How is 'this' pain?"
o "How is 'that' pain?"
o "How is 'the' pain?"
o "how is 'your' pain?"

I overheard a medic asking an old lady (also involved in the accident) in the adjacent cubicle *'how is your pain?'* Her attention was being directed to how much pain she was experiencing with the presupposition (powerful hypnotic language) that the pain belonged to her.

Within a few minutes of me being present with my full attention, while carrying the congruent intention to reassure his Reptilian Brain that it was safe, Chris' essential monitor readings, at least the ones I could track (oxygen level, heart rate and blood pressure), improved significantly. Enough for me to return to the task in hand; ringing his parents.

All the boys were released from hospital within a week and made full recoveries.

We want to help children and adults learn how to direct their 'attention' and get clarity of their intention. It's like shining a spotlight inside their brain. We can do this conversationally and through play.

Case Study: Zac's trap

15-year-old Zac was given various labels (ASD, dyspraxia) that specified emotional immaturity and re-activeness. We soon figured that he could use his smart Thinking Mind to shift some of the feelings that were holding him back. This was not his first appointment, so we had already established rapport and some basic skills.

We started the session with our focus in his Reptilian Brain, using a drum to generate rhythms of movement and shifting balance, moving limbs and adding some 'cross hemisphere' movements like left elbow to right knee and vice versa.

Then we sat still and did some **Nostril Breathing** to regulate oxygen-carbon dioxide exchange and remind him of the technique to reduce stress. To do this, *cover the right nostril with the right thumb and breathe in through the left nostril, cover the left nostril with the right index finger and breathe out through the right nostril, then breathe in through the same (right) nostril, before breathing out through the left nostril. Repeat for a few minutes. This helps to activate and oxygenate both hemispheres because each nostril functions independently to activate cranial nerves from both hemispheres.*

Then we were ready to turn attention to Zac's **feeling** Mammalian Brain and began exploring things that he saw and heard that made him feel happy and unhappy (using the PES scale 1-10 and a list of words that describe feelings). The context was 'at school'. This is what was revealed:

SEE	THINK	FEEL (1-10)	FEEL (DESCRIPTOR)
History - WW2	"I'm going to learn something new"	9	Excited

HEAR	THINK	FEEL (1-10)	FEEL (DESCRIPTOR)
"Go to lunch"	"I'm going to see my friends"	7	Happy

SEE	THINK	FEEL (1-10)	FEEL (DESCRIPTOR)
Maths equations	"This will be difficult"	3	Tired

HEAR	THINK	FEEL (1-10)	FEEL (DESCRIPTOR)
"It's P.E."	"It's going to be hard"	4	Embarrassed

We then talked about using his smart Thinking Mind to change the feelings from *tired* and *embarrassed* into something better – he agreed. Using the whiteboard, we drew out a thinking process that could change the feeling associated with maths – we re-framed meaning: **"this will be difficult".**

Initially, Zac said he thought **all** of maths will be difficult. Then (after I had lightly challenged the generalisation) he conceded that **some** of maths will be difficult. Then I asked him to run his **timeline forward** a bit and understand *why* he was doing maths – he concluded that he was very motivated to pass his maths GCSE.

So, we amended the sentence: ~~"this will be difficult"~~ and replaced it with: ***Some of maths will be difficult – but I want to pass my GCSE*** (the word '*but*' places conscious attention on the second half of any sentence).

I asked him if he and his teachers believed he had the capability to understand maths more and he said yes, so we further amended the sentence: ***Some of maths will be difficult – but I want to pass my GCSE – and I have the capability to understand maths more*** (the word '*and*', keeps the attention flowing forward and the term '*more*' is open-ended and non-specific).

I asked him what he thought a solution (to understanding maths better) might be and he replied, '*asking for help when I don't understand*'.

'Some of maths will be difficult – but - I want to pass my GCSE – and – I have the capability to understand maths more – and ask for help when I don't understand' (now his brain had something to aim towards rather than feeling trapped).

SEE	THINK	FEEL (1-10)	FEEL (DESCRIPTOR)
Maths equations	"Some of maths will be difficult – but - I want to pass my GCSE – and – I have the capability to understand maths more – and - ask for help when I don't understand".	9	Confident

Next, we looked at re-framing his thoughts about PE: *"It's going to be hard".*
I drilled into the detail a bit to clarify a few things such as what he was really referring to, and rugby came out as the real problem for him because he didn't like playing rough games.

He was afraid of being hurt and embarrassed that his physical co-ordination wasn't as good as he wanted it to be. He didn't like feeling different from others.

He was particularly afraid of tackles and shared his strategy for 'staying back a bit and not having to actually get into a tackle'. He was happy with his strategy, but then felt cross/embarrassed with the thought that he 'should' be getting into tackles.

Following the same process as with maths, we used the whiteboard to **re-organise and re-framed the words from his head** so that he could find a nicer feeling, eventually reaching a statement that he was happy with:
In real terms, if he feels good and brave, he's actually more likely to engage in the game with more ease.

93

HEAR	THINK	FEEL (1-10)	FEEL (DESCRIPTOR)
"It's P.E."	"I don't like rough games – but – I have to play rugby – so - I've got a good method and tactic for keeping safe in PE."	9	Brave

This is a simple example of building a narrative that will support learning.

To the mind that is still, the whole universe surrenders

LAO TZU
ANCIENT CHINESE PHILOSOPHER

Not thinking at all
Switching off the Thinking Mind can be a wonderful restorative treat to the whole brain. It interrupts 'top-down' thinking patterns and restores 'bottom-up' coherence.

Summary: The Principle of Clarity
The Thinking Mind is the creator of narratives that 'make sense' of experience and help decide where to place 'attention'.

Any rational, thinking, planning and judging brain goes 'off-line' during a Survival brain reaction.

Words that trigger Stress emotions are easy to habituate as scripts, while poor clarity of brain aim can keep the brain in a state of dissonance.

The executive control centre can drive peak physical, emotional and mental outputs. It needs self-awareness and clarity to orchestrate whole brain power and performance for Thrive.

BEFORE WE MOVE ON, PLEASE CAPTURE YOUR THOUGHTS:

» Questions

» Comments

» Insights

CHAPTER FIVE

"If you have built castles in the air, your work need not be lost... Now put the foundations under them"

HENRY DAVID THOREAU

ESSAYIST, POET, PHILOSOPHER (1817-1862)

CHAPTER FIVE: THE SECRET INGREDIENT

In previous chapters, we have explored the Reptilian, Mammalian and Thinking brains and looked at three key brain states - Survive, Stress and Thrive. Now, we look at the secret ingredient in helping you to identify how to help someone who is 'stuck' - Happy Brain™ Basic Needs.

We have now explored the brain as three regions - Reptilian, Mammalian and Thinking brains. We have also looked at three key brain states - Survive, Stress and Thrive. We summarise that the Stress brain can activate or mimic Survive and that resilience happens when it opts for Thrive.

To do this, we need to get an indication which brain part is acting as a sort of **prime mover,** i.e. triggering a reaction or flow of thoughts, feelings and behaviours that will result in either Thrive or Survive. Our model helps us to perceive which aspects of the brain are:

o   Balanced/balancing

o   Out of kilter

Thus, we are always looking for clues about which brain part to address first, i.e. should we start by addressing actions, feelings or words? Should we:

»   **Drive** insights through questions that lead to self-awareness
»   **Direct** and influence a different emotional state
»   **Distract** behaviour with new actions

Knowing when, where, what and how to help someone who is stuck or struggling can be tricky, and in this chapter, we provide you with specific tools to help you identify where to start and where to go next.

HAPPY BRAIN™ BASIC NEEDS

When we seem to sabotage our goals, or we notice that children cannot behave in the way they clearly want to, sometimes it's useful to look at what conflict may be occurring between *conscious* and *unconscious* goals. Sometimes, it's as if there is something secret or hidden that drives emotions to produce unwanted behaviours.

To help us get to the bottom of this, I've created something called the Basic Needs; you can also think of these as (unconscious) 'brain goals'.

Brain goals assume that the lower brain regions (that prioritise Survival) are constantly filtering for reasons to take action, and this will always trump any higher 'Thinking' goal.

We are looking to understand the current situation where the quality and/or quantity of our Basic Needs (brain goals) are *met* enough to drive Thrive, or *unmet* enough to create Stress. If enough are *unmet* then the Brain switches to Survive.

Almost all of these 'reasons' for taking action

remain below our radar of awareness, yet once we become conscious of them, we immediately see new behavioural choices.

It is useful to identify Basic Needs that are unmet because they may re-direct or sabotage the intended behaviour. Once we have addressed any deficits, we gain clues about what to do next. Deficits may be:

o   Temporary
o   Acute
o   Chronic
o   Singular
o   Multiple
o   Ingrained

The more a 'deficit' is ingrained, or emotionally flagged as important, the stronger the behavioural urge to recover the unmet need. The opposite is also true.

Take the body's need for water as an example: If your mental map knows a plentiful supply of water, then any signals of absence (thirst) will trigger only mild discomfort.

If, on the other hand, the mental map knows scarcity of water (e.g. drought, neglect or poverty), then *any signals of absence will alert the Stress brain in preparation for the Survival brain to take over* and all focus to divert to finding a source of hydration.

In our coaching kit, the Basic Needs Set consists of wipe-clean cards or small palm-sized discs that support quality conversations around behaviours that strengthen or deplete mental, emotional and physical wellbeing.

As a tool, this set can be used by anyone to direct attention, draw out key information, or embed important learning. Conversations can be as directive or ambiguous as the user wants. In skilled hands (ideally NLP trained) the Basic Needs Set becomes a real power tool.

By the way, our Basic Needs Set is not the same as the psychologist Abraham Maslow's famous Hierarchy of Needs model. Rather, we're looking through a much broader set of filters.

There is no hierarchy; we are looking to understand the current situation where the quality and/or quantity of our Basic Needs, met or unmet, is driving or inhibiting Thrive.

This information provides us with clues to know what to do next *in this moment only*.

Here are the first 15 Basic Needs:

Feeling listened to without judgment.

Talking out loud helps us to straighten out our thoughts and get in touch with personal patterns of emotion. It helps us to connect to inner fears, hopes and desires and contemplate our perspectives of time. When someone listens to us speaking, we feel worthy of their attention, which in turn helps to build self-respect. When someone listens *unconditionally*, we can trust that our narrative won't be corrected, interrupted, humiliated, dismissed or undermined. People who listen may include a therapist, coach, friend, stranger, even a helpline. Listening skills are rarely taught. Helping a child to know and value feeling heard and listened to teaches their brains the *listening pattern* which encourages them to do the same for others.

> » Feeling listened to helps to settle the **Mammalian Brain.**
> » Key neurotransmitter in our super 6: Oxytocin.
> » Key coaching questions:
> When and with whom do you feel listened to?
> What are their listening skills?
> How might you develop your listening skills?

Identity. Who am I?

We need to find a congruence between who we think we are and how the world validates us. We inflate or deflate beliefs about how we are perceived by others and use our personal narrative to convince the world that we are who we want to be, or believe we are. We want to be able to find a script that motivates us to Thrive while still remaining socially acceptable. This is **a think-feel-think-feel** dynamic.

Self-esteem is built by taking useful action towards a desired goal and feeling rewarded through integrity. This Basic Need can connect people to a perceived sense of purpose.

> » Clarity of sense of self helps to settle the **Thinking Mind.**
> » Key neurotransmitter in our super 6: Dopamine.
> » Key coaching questions:
> How do you think your friends and family perceive you?
> Do you feel they see the real you?
> Who is the true-you?
> How might you be truer to yourself?

Connection to and cooperation with others.

We need to belong to a social group and share physical space and Thrive/Survive activities and narratives. We understand ourselves better through responding to the similarity/differences of people around us and being able to give/take feedback for the common good. We thrive when we can be true to ourselves within the group dynamic, where physical touch and active co-operation support social bonding and learning.

» Feeling connected helps to settle the **Mammalian Brain.**

» Key neurotransmitter in our super 6: Oxytocin.

» Key coaching questions:
Among which group of people do you feel most 'you'?
Which activities help you feel connected to others?
Are you a team player or do you prefer hierarchies?
How might you build stronger connections and with whom?

Shelter for physical safety and protection.

We need protection from anything/anyone that could harm us. We need a warm, dry, clean environment. When we feel safe, we can rest and switch on the parasympathetic nervous system. Familiarity is important in this space so that we can predict physical, emotional and mental structures. From this safe space we can go out to explore unpredictable and unfamiliar experiences. Places of safety may include a room, place of worship, a class, social group, therapy room, a person's personal space or a natural environment. Children often define their bedroom as safe territory, and ideally we want 'home' to be a safe haven. We will defend our territory. Some people treat their mental maps as their territory/only place of safety.

» Feeling safe and protected helps to settle the **Reptilian Brain.**

» Key neurotransmitter in our super 6: Serotonin.

» Key coaching questions: In which physical space do you feel safest?
How do you nurture a safe haven for yourself or for others?
What do you feel territorial about? How might you build stronger boundaries & with whom?

Asking questions without feeling judged.

We have to make a decision to ask a question. Some people ask questions to 'gather' information. Other people ask questions to seize 'air space' and assert their opinions, some ask questions to attract attention, or to confirm what they have already assumed.

Asking good quality and purposeful questions is a vital communication skill.

Not asking questions prevents us learning. Thinking Traps are a barrier to gathering good quality Thrive information.

> » Asking well-targeted questions boosts confidence, which helps to settle the **Thinking Mind.**
> » Key neurotransmitter in our super 6: Dopamine.
> » Key coaching questions: When (typically) do you ask good quality questions?
> Before asking a question, are you usually clear about its purpose?
> How might you get better clarity of purpose before asking a question?

Movement for self-expression and energy release.

Our bodies are made for movement. The nervous system continually carries signals to the cardiovascular and endocrine systems, to muscles, tendons and ligaments, so we can mobilise joints and pull or push levers (bones) to generate movement.

If we do not move, or we move beyond our capabilities, our bodies will signal a Stress reaction. We move to discharge excess energy and to express our inner world.

> » Physical movement helps to settle the **Reptilian Brain.**
> » Key neurotransmitter in our super 6: Endorphin.
> » Key coaching questions:
> What type of movement invigorates you?
> How do you know when you need to move and in what form?
> How might you improve the frequency, intensity and variety of your physical movements?

Attachment to significant caregiver.

We all need safe, unconditional physical touch and to experience intimacy within the personal space of a significant human. We need to be able to trust and predict how they will respond and freely ask for or offer touch, for example, hand holding or hugging. Feeling special, safe and loved is a vital component for Thrive. As is defining, maintaining and trusting the boundaries of our personal space, and respecting the same for others. Children who experience poor primary attachments often learn to ricochet in and out of other people's personal space. Pets can be great substitutes for unavailable humans.

» Feeling attached helps to settle the **Reptilian Brain.**
» Key neurotransmitter in our super 6: Oxytocin.
» Key coaching questions: With whom do you feel utterly safe and connected?
How do you ask for intimacy?
To whom do you offer unconditional physical contact?
How might you increase the quality of physical contact with significant others?

Nutrition

Fats, carbohydrates, proteins, vitamins and minerals provide energy, repair, growth and regulation of brain/body chemistry.

We need food to provide fuel for our existence. The enteric nervous system (gut) is often referred to as the 'second brain' and it sends information directly to the brain through the vagus nerve. Over 30 neurotransmitters are found in the enteric nervous systems and 95% of the body's serotonin is produced and stored in the gut. Everything we ingest will have a profound effect on physical, emotional and mental wellbeing.

» Good nutrition helps to settle the **Reptilian Brain.**
» Key neurotransmitter in our super 6: Serotonin.
» Key coaching questions: How aware are you of the nutritional values of what you eat?
Which foods (combinations, quantities and quality) help you feel vibrant and energized?
Which foods deplete your energy?
How might you improve the quality of your nutritional intake?

101

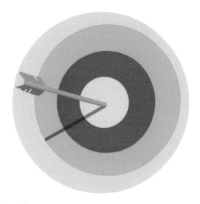

Brain aim

Our brains need a sense of purpose and something to aim towards. In the absence of a conscious goal or direction, we will slip into autopilot (old goals and habits). Old patterns have at some time or another been perceived as rewarding to the unconscious mind. For example, winning an argument might bolster our insecure personal narrative; crying or moaning about life may result in attention or a much-needed hug; battling against the elements to fetch some firewood might help to keep us warm. All behaviours bring some form of reward. We can choose to orientate the brain towards Thrive rewards.

> » Reward helps to settle the **Thinking Mind**.
> » Key neurotransmitter in our super 6: Dopamine.
> » Key coaching questions: How does the behaviour help/hinder Thrive?
> What are the rewards you seek through time, i.e. instant, short-term, medium-term, long-term?
> How might a short-term reward support the long-term plan?

Sleep

During sleep, our brains relax into simple, synchronised, rhythmic waves and restore coherence. Our nervous system needs sleep to balance the neuronal complexities of being awake; re-organising and clearing up neural pathways. Sleeping is vital to Thrive, and sleep deprivation is a major source of Survival states. Equally, Survival states are a major source of sleep deprivation. Stressed thinking can cause havoc with sleep patterns with unsupportive internal dialogues that trigger Stress or even Survival. We all need refreshing, nourishing sleep hygiene and a routine of reducing light and other stimulants to prepare us for rest.

> » Good-quality sleep helps to settle the **Reptilian Brain.**
> » Key neurotransmitter in our super 6: Acetylcholine.
> » Key coaching questions: How do your daytime behaviours (actions, food, drink, etc) affect the quality of sleep? Which bedtime routine settles you best for a good night's sleep? What is the last thing you 'think' before going to sleep? How might you improve the quality of your sleep?

Basic hygiene and age-appropriate self-care of body

and personal space.

This helps to prevent bacteria, fungus and viruses invading the body. Information about someone's hygiene may be subtly received through the senses without having a specific meaning but may trigger an instinctive reaction. Social norms of hygiene help people to feel similar to, and accepted by, their peer group, which supports bonding. Self-awareness of hygiene and self-care are key to Thrive.

- » Basic hygiene helps to settle the **Reptilian** and **Mammalian brains.**
- » Key neurotransmitter in our super 6: Oxytocin.
- » Key coaching questions:
  What for you, is good hygiene?
  What are your main reasons for taking care of yourself?
  How might you improve your personal hygiene?

Hydration

Every cell requires adequate hydration. Good quality electro-chemical signalling inside your brain depends on electrolyte (brain juice) levels and dehydration is a major cause of physical and mental dysfunction which impacts behaviours. A hydrated body has better digestion with easier transportation of nutrients, and a more regulated thermoregulation (body temperature). We can hydrate by drinking more water and eating vegetables and fruit with high water content, and avoiding sugary drinks or diuretics like coffee. Dehydration can cause Survival-type symptoms and inhibit Thrive.

- » Hydration helps to settle the **Reptilian Brain**.
- » Key neurotransmitter in our super 6: Serotonin.
- » Key coaching questions: How does your fluid intake affect the colour of urine and consistency of stools?
  How does your fluid intake affect your physical capability, emotional levels and cognitive function?
  How might you increase the quantity and quality of your hydration levels?

103

What we wear

We need functional clothing to keep us warm, comfortable and protected. Beyond that, our style of clothing helps to position us socially and may make a statement of our identity; we all make subjective assessments about each other. Many people conform to or rebel against fashion trends; both are strong social statements.

» What we wear helps to settle the **Mammalian Brain.**

» Key neurotransmitter in our super 6: Serotonin.

» Key coaching questions: What are your beliefs about people who dress to impress?
How do you choose what to wear each day?
Does your appearance influence your confidence or ability?
How might you dress differently if no-one else was around?

Absence of illness

Our first defences against viruses, bacteria and toxins are the skin, gut lining and airways. Our immune system then eliminates the threat or we seek medical help. When the immune system is compromised by illness, the body becomes defensive and under Stress. Low-grade, chronic or unseen illnesses can also agitate states of Stress. Medications may cause Stress through side effects that unsettle brain-body balance. Placebo (believing yourself well) is well documented for its miraculous effect, as is nocebo (believing yourself unwell). Therefore, our beliefs about illness can cause Stress or contribute to healing.

» Absence of illness helps to settle the **Reptilian Brain.**

» Key neurotransmitter in our super 6: Acetylcholine.

» Key coaching questions: What are your beliefs about your health? How does your immune system deal with minor viruses, bacteria or toxins? What is your first thought when you get a cold? Do you trust your body to self-heal (and know when to seek medical help)? How might you monitor the relationship between minor illness and your thoughts and feelings?

Nature

We are surrounded by electro-magnetic fields that can agitate or soothe us. Some are natural and some are man-made. Nature provides a wonderful antidote to feeling 'Stressed'. Sunlight stimulates vitamin D for strong bones and skin. Fresh, pure air cleanses the cardiovascular system and helps to lower levels of Stress chemistry. Seawater is rich in minerals and is anti-inflammatory. Being in woodland is shown to reduce anxiety and walking barefoot literally grounds our energy systems that equalise with the earth through the exchange of electrons. Sounds of nature soothe us and each sensory channel is stimulated to Thrive.

» Being in nature helps to settle the **Reptilian Brain.**
» Key neurotransmitter in our super 6: Serotonin.
» Key coaching questions: How often do you make it a priority to be grounded in nature?
What are your beliefs about people who do this?
How do you interact with nature, through which senses?
How do you imagine a perfect day in nature?

I have found that at any one time, a child's brain holds a bundle of these Basic Needs MET or UNMET and exploring this can help us understand how their behaviour is being driven.

For example, if a child arrives (at school, an event or a session with me) with a bundle of Basic Needs MET, they are likely to be open to a full sensory experience of the day's events with a (Thrive) brain primed for learning new things, e.g. the curriculum.

However, if a child arrives (at school, an event or a session with me) with a bundle of Basic Needs UNMET, they are likely to be closed to a full sensory experience of the day's events with a (semi-Survival) brain primed to seek what is missing from their Basic Needs bundle. The child's attention is now focused on the unconscious intention to meet the deficit from the environment and people around them. These behaviours can become labelled as 'naughty, clingy, disruptive, or fidgety', which is unfair and damaging to their identity and their peers' perception, which further depletes their Basic Needs bundle.

When working in schools, I like to have children co-operate in small groups to agree an 'order' or hierarchy to the Basic Needs images. This helps me to see/hear their beliefs about the importance of these, as well as calibrating (gauging) their co-operation skills. When working with adults, the simplicity of these images takes serious brains to new places, and I'm always surprised and delighted by the conversation that grow out of addressing these 'brain goals'.

Summary: Basic Needs

In this chapter, we have explored how our brains constantly juggle and prioritise reasons to take action, usually without conscious awareness.

Conversations with open-ended questions stimulated by the pictures (like the examples in this chapter) can produce amazing insights and self-awareness into the holistic wellbeing of a child. Well-targeted questions then reveal valuable information that can help us to make better quality and quantity decisions about building new strategies to support Thrive.

BEFORE WE MOVE ON, PLEASE CAPTURE YOUR THOUGHTS:

» Questions
» Comments
» Insights

CHAPTER SIX

"While complying can be an effective strategy for physical survival, it's a lousy one for personal fulfilment"

DANIEL H PINK

AUTHOR (1964 -)

CHAPTER SIX: MOTIVATION

We've looked at how the brain is motivated to take action consciously and unconsciously. Now, we look at how we might be motivated to do things *differently*.

In the previous chapters, we've explored how the brain is motivated to take action towards reward and away from pain (physical and emotional). These actions may be unconscious or conscious decisions. In the last chapter, we looked at some Basic Brain Needs that act as subconscious motivators.

Motivation is a 'feeling' that tells us what to do/not do. I like to make a distinction between *motivation* and *compliance*, because one is self-determined and the other is connected to conforming:

Motivation comes from a self-determined feeling that produces energy to take action *towards* a reward.

Compliance comes from a need to *conform* to the needs of others.

Everyone is motivated to do *something*!
The question we need to address is - motivated to do what? And why?

We are motivated *to get away from* danger/predators, and motivated *to seek* food, water, the attention of certain others and attract a mate. We are motivated to empty our bladders and bowels. We are motivated to predict the patterns of the people, places and things in our world. We are motivated to maintain our Basic Needs (*last chapter*).

As a very young child, you were motivated by instinct. And then by the rewards of your social group. What did you learn? Perhaps you learned that speaking out in class brought ridicule (= *bad feeling*) and you lost your motivation to speak openly. Or that praise and adulation felt so good you wanted more. Maybe you learned that comparing yourself to others helped you to work out who to compete with. Or did you learn that building lots of Stress gave you the tidal wave of *oomph* to get up and go?

Remember a time when you couldn't wait for something special to happen and you were so excited you could hardly eat? Kids naturally tremble and squeal, jump up and down and speak super-fast when they are excited. Their systems are primed for lots of activity and we often talk about the endless energy of childhood days.

Try this: Imagine you are trembling with excitement, so much so that you want to squeal, jump up and down and speak super-fast? How do you feel now? The chances are, you feel uncomfortable, especially if you've been conditioned to suppress the expression of overt signs of excitement; which is fine, except the energy is still surging and needs to be used.

Since being a young child, I have always loved public speaking, debating, amateur dramatics; I liked a big enough audience to match the feelings inside that I would otherwise keep in. But when I stand up before an audience, I still tremble in the first few minutes as my rational filters go through default patterns of self-awareness and self-protection (perceiving the judgements of others) that I've acquired over time. That's OK, my brain is doing its job and I know how to help it do its best.

Motivating others

Why do we seek to motivate others? Because they ask for help? Because we know what's good for them? Or so we get to feel in control? Because we want something done? For a collective good? Is '*motivating*' others any different to '*influencing*' others? Or '*manipulating*' others? I believe these are important questions to ask yourself - '***why do I want this person to do something differently?***'

With children, we have to balance the individual motivational needs with those of a family/class/group. I hear parents trying to convince teenagers to tidy their room by bribing with money or threatening withdrawal of privileges, e.g. internet access. The parents perceive these are good strategies, and they may be, but only to achieve *compliance* (neurologically) by teaching the teen to either obey authority, or rebel. It doesn't teach them how to drive their own brains towards *self-determined* goals. At best (as a parent of teenagers), you can try to connect your goal to something of value to them, e.g., "*When your room is tidy, you can have your mates round...*" which, if delivered congruently and without emotion, might work.

Both *motivation* and *compliance* are valid processes along the way, but unless your child is joining the military (where compliance is the only option for survival) you really don't want to be teaching them to comply without engaging their clarity of thinking and purpose.

Think that through - do you want your teenage child feeling that they 'should' do something they don't really want to do, just because they've become *conditioned to comply to the instructions of a dominant other?*

Think about that myriad of consequences! Do you want your teenager to have sex, take drugs, self-harm, commit crime etc., without having the skills to think it through and be clear about their motivation? **We want to teach children to have the skills and self-confidence to evaluate the consequences of their personal choices.**

A frequent mistake I see, is where parents and teachers aim a child's mind towards fear of failing in an effort to drum up some (reverse psychology) 'motivation'. For example, a parent might say: *'I reckon you are going to fail that test'*, which could be translated as:

o Statement of truth (intention to be honest)
o Statement of worry (intention to prevent disappointment)
o Statement of projection (intention to feel good by putting another down)
o Statement of reversed psychology (intention to kickstart an opposing reaction)
o Statement to test reaction (intention to judge response)

That parent is offering a smorgasbord of unnecessarily confusing patterns to the child's brain. What a waste of (both parent and child) energy! A 'cleaner' statement might be: *'I believe you'll do*

your best - how may I help?' which leaves the child responsible for building/modifying their own patterns, bolstered by the knowledge that someone believes in their abilities while knowing support is available. And trusting them to deal with whatever the outcome turns out to be.

Even if fear of failure has become your personal habitual driver of motivation (do you leap out of bed after the fourth alarm, filled with anxiety because you're now late, but 'motivated' to finally get up?), it really isn't the best one for your child.

Many years ago, when I taught trampolining students to forward somersault, many would tilt their shoulders at the last minute and rotate around the wrong axis, landing awkwardly.

This is because when you aim towards something you are afraid of, your instinct brain takes over and your eyes need to look away at the last minute; in this case tilting the head/shoulders and altering the axis of rotation.

We want to avoid a single mode of motivation where children only fear failure, because in this case they run the risk of always looking away and never trying. One tip is to **help them to aim their attention towards imagined good feelings in their future, connected to their desired outcome.**

Another frequent mistake is to assume your child is motivated by the same values as you. A teenager motivated by having their friends round may not be encouraged to tidy their room by losing pocket money (just because money is important to you) but may instead value having their friends round.

Finding out what other people value is a great bonding exercise. Do you know what the highest values of your nearest and dearest are?

Evaluation notes: Happy Brain™ Assistant during a school visit

The kids were asked to write down what they'd liked doing best, and what they'd noticed their friends enjoying. Some had a bit of trouble remembering the different things they'd done during the day, but on the whole they all managed to remember something.

The approaches to "what my friends enjoyed" were interesting. Some kids had no trouble remembering what their friends had enjoyed (mostly the girls found this easy). Some other kids asked around their tables - "what did you enjoy?" and found their answers this way.

*One boy told me that, **because he hadn't known that he would have to remember what he thought his friends had liked; he hadn't taken any notice** of what they had enjoyed. I asked him to remember the things we'd done and if he'd seen any other kids laughing or smiling. He then remembered a few examples.*

When we did an activity looking at behaviours that the kids liked, they did this on their own, and wrote down their answers. I went around to see how they were getting on, and I was surprised that the most common problem area was "My behaviours that I like". The kids found it hard to think of things that they themselves do that they like.

Some of the teachers said that they wanted examples of how to use these processes in other areas of teaching/ cross-curricular. Perhaps a teacher's manual with some written examples would satisfy this.

Presupposing success

You can help to motivate a child by using language that presupposes their desired success. This directs their attention to follow neural pathways that are easy to access. For example:

"*When you have done your homework then we can play a game.*"

When presupposes the homework will be done, followed by a reward; this keeps the brain running smoothly.

Unlike this example:

"*If you do your homework, then we can play a game.*"

Because **if** presupposes a **choice** of action, which is confusing when homework isn't really a choice.

Now think about where you can **drive someone's attention** using the following statements:

o   "*What was the best thing about your day?*"
o   "*How was your day?*"
o   "*Was anyone mean to you today?*"
o   "*I hope you sleep well*"
o   "*I hope you have lovely dreams*"
o   "*I hope you don't have any more nightmares*"
o   "*What are you most looking forward to next weekend?*"
o   "*Are you looking forward to next weekend?*"
o   "*Are you dreading next weekend?*"

Each statement directs attention to connect different internal pictures, sounds and associated feelings. Make sure you are directing someone else's brain on purpose, with integrity, and supporting their neurological capacity to Thrive.

Case Study: Being a mind detective

Susi was a 15-year-old struggling with maths. She was very demotivated in this subject, and together we explored how she 'managed' her motivation. She explained that some of the maths questions were really hard to figure out (I agreed with her, by the way, they were confusing!). We looked at the process of accessing her knowledge and how the quality of her inquiry (to self) questions changed her motivation:

Me: *"When you read a maths question – what do you ask yourself?"*
Susi: *"What do they want me to do?"*
This told me that Susi was confusing herself by trying to please the teacher rather than improve her maths capability.
I suggested a new, smarter question:
"How can I solve this?"
'*How*' told Susi's brain that she could answer the question and linked to her love of doing puzzles, which made her feel happier and more confident.

Another old question: *"How do they want me to answer this?"* made Susi feel uncertain and removed any fun in solving the problem. I suggested a smarter question: *"How many clues can I find in this question?"* This feels simpler and told her brain that the clues were right in front of her.
Another old question: ***"How do I start answering this?"*** felt like an obstacle. I suggested a new smarter question: *"What is clue number 1, 2, 3,"* etc
She could make notes about each **clue** and join them up to answer the question.

Evaluation notes: Happy Brain™ Assistant during a school visit

In praise of curiosity...
Environments I like (classroom, playground, etc.)
We did this as a class activity, Kay choosing kids with their hands up to give an example of environments that they liked. The class had several discussions on whether an offered example was an 'environment' or a 'behaviour'.

One boy put his hand up and said his favourite part of the playground were the monkey bars. Other kids called out that there were no monkey bars in the school playground. The boy said that he'd been thinking about a different playground, not the school playground. Some of the kids around the room started sniggering at his 'mistake'.

Kay then pointed out that which playground was meant by 'playground' wasn't specified. This seemed to be a bit of a revelation to all the kids (the giggling stopped). Some other kids then put their hands up and said that because the word 'playground' was written near the word 'classroom' on the PowerPoint, they had made the association, and made the assumption that 'playground' therefore meant the school playground. Kay praised them for looking for clues around them to solve a puzzle.

Case Study: Motivation

14-year-old Tes was very competitive at home, at school and in sport. For him, typical thoughts that boosted confidence included:

o   *"I'm the best"*

o   *"I'm better than him/her"*

o   *"I'm going to win this (match)"*

Typical thoughts that depleted confidence included:

o   *"I'm not as good as before"*

o   *"I'm not as good as him or her"*

o   *"I'm going to lose this (match)"*

The second type of thinking created disappointment, which in turn led to a Stress brain, poor performance. He was then de-motivated and didn't feel good. He would be really keen to win a tennis match (goal) and played well until he perceived he could no longer win, then swiftly lost the match before entering hours of anger, rumination and blame (of self and others). Here are some of the notes I sent to him after a session when we looked at the success strategies of peak performers:

Hi Tes,

The good news is that when you develop a different 'mindset' - like one that champion sports people use – you get to stay feeling motivated. It's all about changing the goal, and here's how to do it:

First of all, know the difference between a short-term goal and a long-term goal.

A short-term goal might be to eat a snack because you're hungry, whereas a long-term goal might be to have a healthy body.

If you only focus on the short-term goal, i.e., to satisfy hunger, you could easily eat lots of unhealthy foods every time. This may be OK in the short-term, but can have disastrous long-term consequences for health.

Smart people teach their brains to link short-term goals to longer-term rewards.

So, you can see that 'winning the tennis match' is a short-term goal. And becoming a champion tennis player is a long-term goal.

*In the past, you were letting feelings of disappointment de-motivate you. Now we've researched **how** world-class sportspeople stay motivated and we've started to **train your mind** to think like them.*

*Champion sportspeople stay motivated by asking themselves **"how much more can I improve my performance?"** rather than "how can I win the match".*

*A great question to ask yourself is **"how well can I play next time?"** or even **"how much fun can I have** *playing tennis next time?"* I know you have taken your sport very seriously, but did you know that having fun creates powerful brain chemistry that helps your mind and body learn and perform more easily?

Mental rehearsal is key

Using your imagination – on purpose – is a really smart way to improve your performance and success. Here's how: Close your eyes and imagine yourself playing your next sports match (or other performance). See yourself performing effortlessly and easily moving your body around the court, pitch or track; and if you're playing tennis, notice how you serve and return with absolute precision.

*Now use your imagination to **become** that future you, and what do you see? What do you*

hear as the ball rebounds perfectly from the centre of your racquet? How does it feel when your muscles and joints are smooth and powerful?

This is a mental rehearsal that sets your brain towards a useful target, which is to get better at playing tennis.

What next?

There are many ways you can develop your champion mindset, including:

o *Asking yourself 'good and useful questions' to achieve your goals*
o *Taking more tips from world-class performers*
o *Dealing with feedback from others*
o *Switching off unhelpful mind chatter*
o *Developing your Imagineering skills*

Summary: Motivation

We have explored the difference between motivation and compliance and how we are all motivated to move *towards* reward and *away* from pain or fear.

Feeling demotivated is caused by combining the wrong thoughts, feelings, beliefs and actions, resulting in fatigue from holding too much Stress inside. Thrive motivations, on the other hand, feel very rewarding and build champion mindsets and endless energy for action.

In the next chapter, you can explore more case studies that relate to Happy Brain™ clients.

BEFORE WE MOVE ON, PLEASE CAPTURE YOUR THOUGHTS:

» Questions

» Comments

» Insights

CHAPTER SEVEN

"I am not afraid of storms, for I am learning how to sail my ship"

LOUISA MAY ALCOTT
AUTHOR (1832-1888)

CHAPTER SEVEN: FURTHER CASE STUDIES AND CLIENT NOTES

In this chapter, we explore some powerful case studies and client notes which help to bring together and embed all we have learned in the previous chapters.

Case study: The little devil

What a devil of a job I had a few years ago, dealing with a 10-year-old lad who, quite simply, thought he was a 'bad kid'.

Adrian was one of the first kids in Class 5 to catch my attention during a Happy Brain™ Day. He displayed unruly behaviour, shouting out and generally disagreeing with everyone and anything. Physically, he was loose-toned in his movements with his head tilted off towards his left shoulder; he seemed to have little control over his physiology yet was quite tense. Verbally, he was quick and articulate for his age, though his vocabulary was negative and reactive. Emotionally, he seemed upset, defensive/offensive and unable to deal with any perceived unfairness during the day. Emotionally, he seemed to be hurting.

Sometimes, when faced with a prevailing attitude of '*I can't do this, that or anything. And I don't like this, that or anything*', enlisting the objector's help to change their focus of attention is powerful. So I asked Adrian to be one of the demonstrators of a game in our **Calm Confidence Kit** called **Power Up**.

Adrian came to the front of the class and proceeded to do the opposite of everything I asked of him. I joked and moved on. "*Thank you, Adrian, you can sit down now...*" I gestured for him to join the seated class. He sat down on the very spot he had been standing. "*Well you said sit down,*" he challenged, almost as if he chose a literal interpretation of my instruction as a weapon

of mass obstruction! We joked and moved on. Note: I suspected this was his behavioural stance rather than true literal interpretation, which of course some children do make.

"*He used to be fine, until Year 2,*" confided the teacher during lunch break. "*Something seemed to change around that time, and he has become a very naughty boy.*" I made a mental note of the teacher's belief and narrative that he was '*a naughty boy*', because if Adrian continued to be labelled as such, his identity, and educational and social potential would be compromised.

After lunch, the final Happy Brain™ activity was to have the children visualise what their brains might look like inside. This exercise is metaphoric, creative, expressive, and a celebration of uniqueness.

Once a clear image, sound or feeling was imagined, the children each began drawing their personalised Happy Brain™, and the class soon got busy with colours, shapes, patterns, words and illustrations. As a general observation, the girls seemed to mostly draw pastel-coloured hearts inside their imaginary brains, with friendship and love compartments. The boys appeared to favour pulleys, levers and earthy tones. Adrian drew a brain which was spiky around the top and outer edges and then sat back in his chair, crossed his arms, and announced, "*I can't do this.*"

Sitting alongside him for a while, I found my first opportunity to work one-to-one with him. Building

116

rapport, at first I stayed entirely within his reality, a skill often referred to as 'pacing'. We chatted about his 'brain' under the mantle of me being a mind coach. I was curious, interested, and I gently began to lead his attention using NLP Milton Model language, which focuses on artfully vague suggestions. "*What, until now, has stopped you drawing your brain?*" I asked.

That powerful phrase, '*until now*', seemed to work, as he appeared deep in thought for a moment before revealing a nugget of key information:

"*I have the devil inside me,*" he replied.

Note: Many parents, teachers, adults, or friends would tell him not to be silly or that he was wrong. Others may even agree with him. In fact, you might observe your own response to that statement. But we do not pay so much attention to the *words* in these situations; Adrian was simply stating his belief – the nugget that becomes a *key* to transformation.

"*Cooool,*" I said, as he gave me a look of suspicion. "*So where, on the paper, will you draw that little red guy?*"

Now at this stage, I most wanted to validate his narrative and belief in order to stay in rapport, but at the same time I used magical Milton Model language to begin to trick his mind. "*That little red guy*" did the trick.

The word '*that*' is such a simple way to begin to dissociate someone from a picture inside their head. We can move the picture closer by saying '*this*' picture or move it further away by saying '*that*' picture. And when saying "*little – red – guy*" I changed my intonation to make other changes inside Adrian's imagination. The scary thing was now being referred to as a *little*, *red* and a *guy*. Matter of fact.

Suddenly, Adrian jolted forward into full drawing mode, released from whatever thoughts had been holding him stuck. Note: Sometimes, to change the emotional state of the person feeling helpless or stuck, all we need to do is give their neurological map somewhere different to go. Certainly, Adrian had now adopted a new, engaged manner; for the first time all day, he was focused and on-task, and a red, devil-like figure began to emerge on the paper in front of him. The illustration included a pitchfork, a black cloud, rain and lightning.

He sat back and gave me a confused look that seemed to ask a question and answer a fear simultaneously. "*I told you so...*"

"*But where is the balancer?*" I asked, explaining some basic physics about opposing parts. More language magic – my statement left no room for him to disagree because it not only *presupposed* there was a balancer, it was also backed up by science, should he need any *convincer*.

I waited until his eyes stopped moving around (we call these 'eye-accessing cues') as he was searching inside his mind for 'the balancer'.

He found it!

"*A golden angel,*" he said, "*with golden sunshine beaming down*".

And at that very moment his little face illuminated, as I gently touched his left shoulder, smiled and made a strong sound of '*wowwwwwwww*' (this is multi-sensory anchoring to give his brain a new message; happy feelings and happy thoughts are the way to go!). It was a moment of delight. He had discovered something that had previously escaped his awareness, and he now freely drew his 'balancer' with great focus, care and attention.

Together we admired the new brain picture showing two equal-sized compartments balanced inside his brain; at last, his obstacles removed, he was free to draw a full and complete drawing, just like the other children.

"Didn't you know?" I asked in a surprised voice, *"we all have something just like that little red guy and the golden angel inside our minds. It's just knowing where to look inside your mind."*

I shifted my language into *dissociated past tense* when referring to *'that'* little red guy (devil) and into *associated present/future* for *'this'* golden angel. Adrian seemed calmer and less tense, and asked if he could show his drawing to the class – for the first time all day he offered a positive contribution.

As the session ended, the children assembled on the mat at the front of class, all holding their wonderful and various pictures of their Happy Brain™. I asked Adrian to be my first 'sharer' at the front of the class, and as he began to quietly and methodically describe the imagined workings of his mind, I gently reminded his nervous system of the good feelings we had associated to the discovery of the golden angel by gently re-touching the spot on his left shoulder where I had previously touched as I said *'wowwwwwwwww'*, which I repeated in the same tone as earlier.

The children and teachers listened intently as he described how he had felt opposing parts inside his brain - a devil and an angel.

"Put your hand up if you have ever experienced something just like that little red guy [pointing to the devil on the paper] *inside your mind,"* I instructed the class, lifting my own arm straight up in the air.

As a sea of hands rose in front of us, Adrian's face flushed as he beamed a beautiful smile. I suspect that until that moment, he had *believed* he was a little devil.

The class teacher and I also shared our experience of feeling, *"something like that little red guy inside our heads sometimes"* even as grown-ups. Then we chatted as a class about the idea of other balancers inside our heads. *"How many of you can ride a bike?"* I asked the class. Most of the class said yes. *"How many of you could ride a bike when you were aged two?"* No hands were raised. *"So how did you get good at it?"*
"Practice!" They called in chorus.
"Good point," I said, *"because we know that whatever you practise, you get good at. So let's practise looking for balancers inside our minds, shall we?"* A resounding *'yes'* was the reply.

I asked Adrian which behaviours he might like to practise more of - the behaviours of *that* little red guy or the behaviours of *this* angel. Note here the continued use of *this* and *that*, and the separation of *behaviour* from *identity*. *"The angel,"* he beamed. And I invited him to think about what that would look, sound and feel like. I explained to the class that it is quite 'normal' to feel ideas of naughtiness pop up sometimes, but smart kids (like them) learn to look at their mind's balancer and at least consider they have another choice; a *balancer* choice.

Concluding the day's activities with the class, I asked them to imagine floating forward in time in their imagination and visit themselves two weeks from now. I asked them:

o What improved behaviours have they noticed in each other?
o How much smarter and happier have they become?

118

Adrian was now upright, symmetrical, smiling and appeared much stronger and happier than he had been earlier that day

Of course, in this situation, I didn't get to influence the system he lives in: home, school, family, friends, teachers and others. But I did get to challenge a limiting belief that had been holding him back.

Here is our representation of his drawing:

Due to copyright law, we cannot show you the actual drawings, but here you can see our interpretation of what the kids have shown us as they visualise their brains in unique ways. This teaches them to be OK with difference:

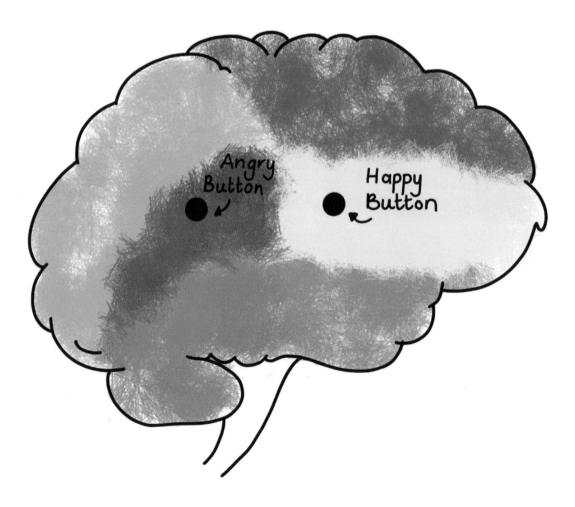

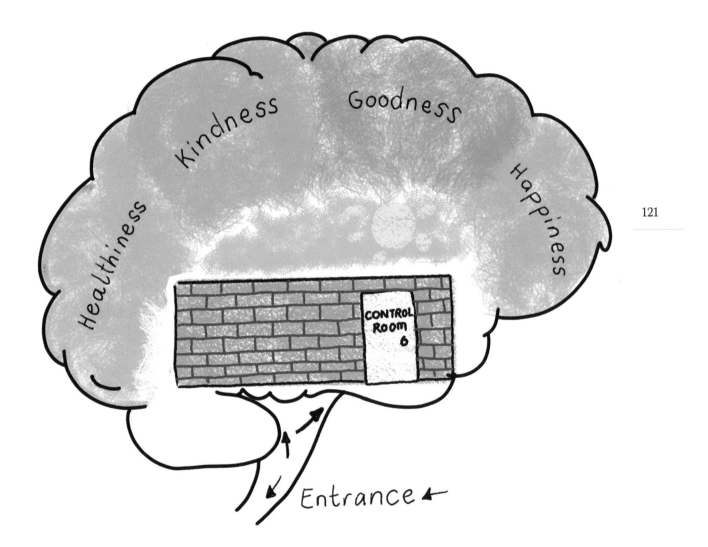

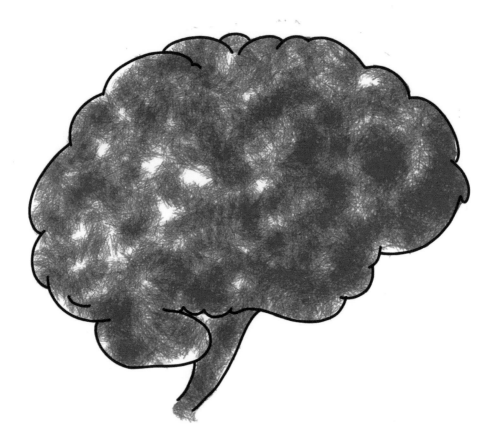

This is a representation of a drawing by a child who was distressed after realising the other kids on his table had all used different colours, shapes and words for their brain drawing. He felt especially 'different', the odd one out.

I sat with him and explored all the textures he had created by using different pressures and intensities. I encouraged him to look at the individual line directions and differing gaps between them and we wondered about the hidden patterns that only he could see. There is always so much more to explore.

Case Study: Undoing think traps

16-year-old Henry has a diagnosis of Asperger Syndrome (also known as Asperger's), and in this session we worked to 'stretch' some of his *thinking traps*. The results show how we can develop and expand thinking.

I handed Henry a pack of cards showing photos of facial expressions with descriptive words. I asked him to look through them, thus assessing his way of 'sorting' through information. His first comments were about the faces that reminded him of someone he knew, indicating an *initial sorting for familiarity, by image rather than word.*

Then I asked him to decide if the words and pictures matched (they're supposed to). He picked out 2 cards that he felt were not good matches, offering excellent observation and even better justifications:
Relaxed face card: *"The eyes looked a bit cross and the mouth is not soft enough"*
Hurt face card: *"The 'dog eyes' looked like he was begging, and the mouth pulled in like he was cross".*

I then suggested 3 scenarios and asked Henry to match the card which *felt* the most appropriate to each statement, as follows:
• *"I hear a loud noise outside my house, and I feel..."*
Afraid Because my heart beats faster
• *"I see the bathroom sink looking dirty and I feel..."*
Disgusted Because I feel sick
• *"A kid at school bumps into me and swears at me and I feel ..."*
Hurt - ?? (no awareness of physiological response)

Next, we added a new layer of what a scenario might mean: What is my *imagination* telling me?'
• *"I hear a loud noise outside my house, and I feel..."*
Afraid - I *imagine* it could be a burglar.
• *"I see the bathroom sink looking dirty and I feel..."*
Disgusted - I *imagine* dripping water and bacteria.
• *"A kid at school bumps into me and swears, I feel ..."*
Hurt - I *imagine* he wants to hurt me or say there is something wrong with me or make fun of me.'

We then looked at *stretching* Henry's thinking around each of these situations:
• *"I hear a loud noise outside my house, and I feel..."*
Afraid - I *imagine* it could be a burglar. *But* I can challenge my imagination (or investigate and figure out the real source of the noise, or ask Mum)
• *"I see the bathroom sink looking dirty and I feel..."*
Disgusted - I *imagine* dripping water and bacteria. *But* I can trust my imagination (act with care, rinse the sink, or ask Mum)
• *"A kid at school bumps into me and swears, I feel ..."*
Hurt - I *imagine* he wants to hurt me or say there is something wrong with me or make fun of me. *But* I can *distract* my imagination (carry on walking and ignore him, or wonder if he is always angry on Tuesdays, or imagine he is blowing smoke through his huge cartoon ears).

The *challenge* and *distract* solutions were entirely Henry's and he demonstrated good awareness of basic thinking mechanics.

123

Client notes: Self-talk (Zoe, 17)

Hi Zoe,

Today we explored feeling nervousness before entering your new classroom.

You shared the thought inside your mind before entering the classroom: "This is going to be difficult", which of course tells your brain to get ready for trouble (Stress) and makes you feel, look and sound defensive, as if you were truly ready for trouble!

This isn't the best way to enter the room or make new friends! I suggested you try a new strategy. We started by erasing the word 'difficult' and instead added, "different, exciting, interesting". So instead of saying to yourself "this is going to be difficult", you can say "this is going to be interesting" or "this is going to be exciting" or "this is going to be different".

Say each of these sentences inside your mind and find the one that gives you the nicest feeling. Once you have this good feeling, remember to spin it around to glue it in place. This is important, because when you speak to yourself in a way that lets you feel good, your brain is open to the new challenges and your voice and body language will relax, making you appear more relaxed and likeable to others.

Case Study: Sensory information

14-year-old Lana was fed up of feeling left out of a group of girls at her new school. Moving schools can be tough at any age and Lana, one term in, was yearning for the feelings she used to associate with her old group of pals.

In truth, she still saw the old gang socially and had actually been quite unhappy with them too, but somehow her brain started having her recall the past friendships as much better than the reality had been.

The new girl group was tight, which she believed meant they had all been friends since being small; compounding her feelings that it was impossible for her to become a part of them. She came to see me, asking for help with her feelings around 'social exclusion'.

We established that a couple of girls in the group were being especially kind and friendly towards her, but this didn't seem to satisfy Lana's needs of belonging to the main group, and she found herself:

o Dismissive of the presenting opportunity to forge new friendships; looking beyond the friendly girls, keeping her sights fixed firmly on the big group
o She had begun fantasising the old school friendship group was perfect, despite this contradicting previous discussions with me
o She felt she had lost something of great value, i.e. being at the centre of a group of friends - forgetting the friendship problems she had previously encountered

o She had interpreted the body language of certain group members as meaning they didn't want to include her
o She felt awkward and self-conscious.

To help her to understand the mind mechanics of *think-feel-do*, we started by exploring:
o **Feelings** Self-conscious and awkward around new girl group
o **Behaviour** Withdrawing/wanting to withdraw from the group's periphery
o **Senses** Perceiving that the group was unsure about her unpredictable behaviour and viewed her with suspicion
o **Thinking** They don't like her
o **Feelings** Sad and lonely, then angry and frustrated when she realised her thoughts and behaviours had been contributing to the situation

Lana was about to discover the key to her happiness was to realise that something triggered the feelings, and that something was her **Thinking Patterns.**

Trigger thoughts included:
o *"Making new friends is hard work and tiring"*
o *"Belonging to a big group is important"*
o *"Real friends listen to me and I can say anything to them"*
o *"My old friends were ideal"*
o *"I miss my old friends"*

Those thoughts triggered the feel-bad strategy to start, running in a loop:
THOUGHT triggers FEELING influencing BEHAVIOUR.

Drilling further into the problem

Lana's friendship goal had been to be popular amongst a large group of girls. *Yet she could never control a goal that requires other people to change.* Trying to do that had been exhausting and frustrating, wasting energy and leading to disappointment in others and feelings of unhappiness.

Exploring solutions

How to help Lana to amend her friendship goal meant feeling relaxed and authentic around new people; interested in them and having fun. In other words, **getting to be in charge of the goal.**

Not only could she control this goal, she would actually reinforce some self-esteem through achievement - like having fun (rather than eroding self-esteem by setting goals that could never be achieved).

Getting Lana to change her Thinking would in turn drive new feelings, and therefore change how she behaved. *Changing the Thinking* is key – it puts her back in control.

» **Experiment**
We explored changing the '*trigger thoughts*' by imagining that she had lost all her friendship memories – all of them (good or bad) - then pitching up at school feeling relaxed and fresh, looking for fun people to get to know and generally feeling happy. She was sure she'd feel happy in this scenario.

» **Feedback**
This tells Lana that the obstacle to feeling those natural responses (*relaxed, fresh, looking for fun people to get to know and generally feel happy*) had been her trigger thoughts, which had simply become habituated.

» **Feed forward**
How to un-habituate the thoughts? We decided to take the approach of catching them – the thoughts - and become aware that they are not truths, just patterns of rehearsed brainwaves and neurochemistry.
And challenging her own Thinking - like expanding all the reasons why someone might have 'closed' body language. We drew up a list: cold, unwell, feeling scared, worried etc, until Lana accepted that she could never really know what another person was really Thinking or feeling.

And if she thought the closed body language meant they didn't like her... guess what? She now had a 'trigger thought' to run a feel-bad strategy.

126

We explored new mind experiments to **discover just how much influence she really has over her thinking and feeling**, which led us to conclude that she could:

Practise thoughts so they become habits, e.g.

o Everyone is unique; some people talk more than they listen, others listen more than they talk

o Friendship groups are dynamic, which means people come and go, behaviours shift and change, feelings rise and fall

o Individual friendships are easiest to build

o Being interested in someone is the best friendship gift you can give

o Value the good friendship skills experienced at the previous school

o Remember what she is *gaining* (not feeling that something has been *lost*)

Activities to do

o Balloon Breathing and Balancing Body & Mind activities

o Keep a diary of things she is grateful for (at least 3 each day) to train her brain to build new thinking lines in her mind

o Look at the friendship group through new eyes – 'what she likes to see, hear, do with the girls'

o Keep a diary of what life skills she is gaining each day, e.g. tolerance, acceptance, curiosity

Conclusion

o Friendships are dynamic.

o Resilient thinking enables children and young adults to make new thinking, feeling and behavioural connections.

127

Case Study: Personal boundaries

This is an email I sent to a young client a few years ago as a summary of our session with some coaching notes. Ben was 12 at the time and having trouble at school with bullies:

Hello Ben,

How nice to meet you today and work with you towards building a strong, resilient machine inside your mind's eye; one which will help you realise new ways to think, feel and behave.

I'd like to start by saying how impressed I am at your willingness to try the mind experiments and learn new skills today.

I asked you the magic wand question – *"if my magic wand could bring you anything, what would you most like to see/hear/feel"* (your solution to the problem).

Your wish: *"I wish all the bullies could just be nice and wouldn't annoy people – everyone would be nice and say, 'you can play with us' and I just want to make friends."*

That felt emotional to say out loud and we discussed allowing the emotions to flow rather than try to block them.

We then looked at the 'wish' – *"I wish all the bullies could just be nice"* as a 'goal to aim your brain towards , and we came across a problem:
We can't change other people!
We can't change the bullies!

Even if we understand their brains are Stressed, which makes their behaviours so mean, we can only change our own thoughts, feelings and behaviours (which will eventually have an impact on others).

So, you made another 'wish' – *"improve my social skills"* - and when I wondered what that would bring

for you, you replied, *"people being nicer to me/not laughing at me."*

This is cool really because you are **looking for a solution.** However, it still involves changing someone else's thoughts, feelings or behaviours - and we can't do that.

So, we looked at your new goal as *"how I want to feel"* at school, because *you can influence these feelings*, as we soon discovered with our mind experiments.

We looked at some written descriptions of feelings, so you could look at feelings you didn't want so much and also identity feelings you do want instead.

You circled words to describe **unwanted feelings:** Depressed, miserable, helpless, misunderstood

You circled words to describe **wanted feelings:** **Joyful,** pleased, tolerant, accepting, **lovable,** **proud,** respected, responsible, protected, forgiving, peaceful, **safe,** carefree, **protective,** thoughtful, forgiven, relaxed, satisfied, intuitive. *- The words in **bold** describe some of your regular feelings, which is always nice to appreciate, isn't it?*

We began some mind experiments to explore new ways to change how you think and feel so you feel strong and powerful inside yourself, regardless of the behaviours and words of people around you.

Your future happiness comes from controlling the pictures and sounds you make inside your head and we experimented with some cool ways to change them. To do this, we used the *Perceived Emotional Scale*, which we also call the PES.

The Happy Brain™ Perceived Emotional Scale (PES)

We were able to 'measure' how your feelings changed after each mind experiment.

You were able to change the picture (of a memory that made you feel bad) in lots of different ways:

- o   Colour / Black & white
- o   Moving / Still
- o   Big / Small
- o   Near / Far

We measured your feeling shift from 3-4-3-5-3-7, showing you how **your 'visual' control can so easily make you feel better or worse – on purpose!**

You were also able to **change the sounds** (of a memory that made you feel bad) in a really fun way: You moved the voice from inside your mind into your thumbnail, looked at it and heard a **ridiculous chipmunk voice.** We also practised doing this without moving your hand out in front of you, so your imagination did all the hard work. This technique had the fastest result - 4–8 - and made you laugh! You dissolved your problems in special brain juice.

Now you know *how* to change your thoughts and your feelings and imagineer some new situations in the future. We practised remembering old situations that used to make you feel angry or sad and then using your mind magic techniques, especially the laughter one, to feel good again. Now no-one will ever know your secret power, but they might notice how you no longer react to the bullies. They will never know that inside your mind **you have begun to build a machine – a control panel that brings you inner strength and mind-power.**

We explored the 'energy' of your new mental power and you liked the feeling of energising it further by spinning it from your mind into your tummy and back up again into your mind.

Remember the invisible power pack and Balloon Breathing.
You can also 'breathe away' the horrid feelings, sounds and pictures.
Remember that as the unpleasant feelings, sounds, and pictures get breathed away, they are replaced by feelings of joy and confidence coming in through your invisible backpack. Feel the strength coming through!

Now, I don't know which technique you'll practise most, or how many times you'll listen to the audio link, but I do know that whatever you practise you will get good at, and I look forward to working with you again soon to build even more mind controls.

129

Case Study: Building useful strategies

10-year old schoolmates Zac and Jack had had an 'incident' in the school playground. To help Zac understand his part to play in this, we drew boxes to represent Zac's

thinking and behaviour:. This was the result:

1.	2.	3.
4. Zac spanked Jack's bottom with his hand.	**5.**	**6.**

We began with the *behaviour* - box 4:

1.	2.	3.
4.	**5.** a) Everyone laughed. b) Jack got angry and shouted rude words.	**6.**

And then the *consequences* of that action in box 5:
And the *impact* of this in 6:

1.	2.	3.
4.	**5.**	**6.** Zac felt upset because Jack shouted at him.

And added that he then realised he had hurt Jack's feelings ...

We explored *intention* in box 2:

1.	**2.** Zac wanted to have some fun and had an idea to smack Jack	3.
4.	**5.**	**6.**

And *what he had been thinking just before* he smacked Jack in box 3:

1.	2.	**3.** a) don't do it (he said his left brain told him that!) b) do it (said his right brain told him that!)
4.	**5.**	**6.**

The simple summary of his *unhelpful strategy* was:

1.	**2.** Zac wanted to have some fun and had an idea to smack Jack	**3.** a) don't do it (he said his left brain told him that!) b) do it (said his right brain told him that!)
4. Zac spanked Jack's bottom with his hand.	**5.** a) Everyone laughed. b) Jack got angry and shouted rude words.	**6.** Zac felt upset because Jack shouted at him.

Zac and I talked through this visual sequencing of his thinking and behaviour. We then explored his intention (to have fun) and discussed new choices, eg. telling a joke or suggesting a game.

Client notes: Dissolving sadness

Dear Annie,

It was good to see you today, I hope you enjoyed our mind experiments? Just to recap – you described a 'sadness' that unexpectedly came over you a few times recently, including when you were on holiday.

I reminded you not to feel disappointed in feeling sadness because it's probably that your brain was processing the difficult period you've just been through, just like how we process our day during dream sleep.

Rather than be afraid or disappointed with the sadness, I wanted you to discover how you can use mind tools to be creative and have fun with the imagery that your mind can produce.

You described the sadness as a feeling of blackness/greyness moving inside and outside that felt like thick butter.

*You described the **opposite** and nicer feeling of happiness that feels like freedom and spaciousness, laughter and brightness.*

We experimented with taking these happy 'codes' 'into' the darkness and breathing warm colours through the black/grey. You blew herself a pathway through the dark colour and began to lighten it up, so the sad energy dissolved and was replaced by warmth and brightness. This is such a cool creative tool and I hope you enjoy using it!

You also explored some other cool creative ways to work into, with and through the darkness, rather than accept it, be overwhelmed or afraid of it.

I'm wondering how many times you're going to use this and how simple and easy it will be for you!

We also explored the 'codes' for feeling strong, confident and 'certain' about things and then **merged** *happiness and confidence so the concrete layers blended with the lightness, freedom and expansiveness – another really smart mind tool.*

Perhaps you also remember my tree metaphor for the difference between feeling happy or flexible (willow tree) and strong/certain (solid oak tree).

I'm now very curious to find out next week which of these tools you have used most and which ones you like best. See you then!

Closing notes

The UK Mental Health Foundation cites good mental health as:

o   The ability to learn
o   The ability to feel, express and manage a range of positive and negative emotions
o   The ability to form and maintain good relationships with others
o   The ability to cope with and manage change and uncertainty

I hope you have found this book a valuable contribution to the world of good mental and emotional health and feel inspired to use some of the ideas, techniques and activities presented on these pages.

Perhaps you would like to train with us and discover how creativity and play with purpose can enrich any neurological map. Maybe you would like to become a Licensed Happy Brain™ Coach or Trainer, or learn more about NLP?

I'm immensely proud of the work we (a small but growing team of us) do to educate young minds and guide the adults who will make the biggest difference to Next-Generation Thinking. Please get in touch or explore **Happy Brain™ - Next-Generation Thinking** on YouTube, Facebook and our website, **www.thehappybrainco.com**

Thank you for reading.

136

Afterword

Kay and the Happy Brain™ model has helped our family immeasurably, and for this I will be grateful until my dying day. Our youngest daughter was sexually abused by our babysitter, who told her he would kill her family and our dogs if she told anyone. After three weeks of increasingly frantic behaviour, she was brave enough to release a tiny piece of information that was akin to a bomb exploding in our home and inside our hearts.

Over the next few weeks, the extent of her ordeal surfaced in the form of frantic behaviour and an increased ability to verbalise her experience. It was every parent's worst nightmare. How would you not fall apart? How do you help your child? How do you protect your other child?

The fallout devastated her older sister, my husband and I. Life was unrecognisable and we were in total free-fall with no lifelines. The police criminal process disallows meaningful therapy, but as soon as we were free to, we worked with Kay both individually and as a family.

18 months post-assault, we have joy in our lives. We sing, we dance, we laugh and we are bursting with love. We're extremely close and know that we are all going to be ok. For a long time, I couldn't see the path to joy. Our youngest still has nightmares, but she is the most positive person I know. She is full of love and hope and joy.

Kay has taught us all how to think differently. We don't have the power to change what happened, but we do have the power to make damned sure it doesn't define us. Our duty to our children is to rise up and live our best life. To hold onto anger and sadness only hurts our family more.

Personally, the first time I met Kay she removed what felt like a rock from the pit of my stomach. I didn't know it was there until it was gone. I could move and breathe freely and hadn't been aware that I was suffocating with pain and grief and the powerlessness of not being able to help my baby.

I had no expectations that we could ever feel ok. The fact that we desperately needed help was the only thing clear to us, but I was seeking help for our children. My husband and I being emotionally ok was the key to our children's resilience. At first, all I could hear was criticism - 'you're not coping and its damaging your children'. How could I do better when I was woken by a screaming terrified child several times a night?

Our healing is in our love and our laughter. Kay has taught us all so much about ourselves and how to heal ourselves and each other. We are eternally grateful.

Pippa, parent

Useful references

Aghajanian, G.K. and Marek, G.J. (1997) *Serotonin induces excitatory postsynaptic potentials in apical dendrites of neocortical pyramidal cells* Neuropharmacology 36: 589–599

McMahon, Darrin M. *The History of Happiness: 400 BC– AD1780* Daedalus Journal, Spring 2004

Bethany, E., Kok, Kimberley A., Coffey, Michael A., Cohn, Lahnna I., Catalino, Tanya., Vacharkulksemsuk, Sara B., Algoe, Mary Brantley, and Barbara L. Fredrickson *How Positive Emotions Build Physical Health: Perceived Positive Social Connections Account for the Upward Spiral Between Positive Emotions and Vagal Tone*
Psychological Science (first pub'd May 6, 2013)
DOI: 10.1177/0956797612460827

Brown R.P., Gerbarg PL., J Altern Complement Med *Yogic breathing in the treatment of stress, anxiety, and depression: part 1 – neuropsychologic model* 2005 Feb;11(1):189-201. Review

Carey, J., Churches, R., Hutchinson, G., Jones, J., Tosey, P. (2009) *Neuro Linguistic Programming and learning: teacher case studies on the impact of NLP in education* CfBT Education Trust

Dahlgren, G., & Whitehead, M. (1993) *Tackling inequalities in health: What can we learn from what has been tried?* Background paper for The King's Fund International Seminar on Tackling Health Inequalities. Ditchley Park, Oxford: The King's Fund.

Gutman, L., Joshi, H., Parsonage, M., & Schoon, I. (2015) *Children of the new century: Mental health findings from the Millennium Cohort Study* London: Centre for Mental Health

Igor Grossmann, Baliinder, K., Sahdra and Joseph Ciarrochi *A Heart and A Mind: Self distancing Facilitates the Association Between Heart Rate Variability and Wise Reasoning* Frontiers in Behavioural Neuroscience (first pub'd: April 8, 2016) DOI: 10.3389/fnbeh.2016.00068

Knapp M. (2003) *Hidden costs of mental illness* Br. J. Psychiatry 183:477-478

Kraus T., Hosl K., Kiess O., Schanze A., Kornhuber J., Forster C. *BOLD fMRI deactivation of limbic and temporal brain structures and mood enhancing effect by transcutaneous vagus nerve stimulation* J Neural Transm. 2007;114:1485–93.

Lazar, S.W., Bush G., Gollub R.L., Fricchione G.L., Khalsa G., Benson H. *Functional brain mapping of the relaxation response and meditation* Neuroreport. 2000;11:1581–5.

Marijke De Couk, Ralf Caers, Liza Musch, Johanna Fliegauf, Antonio Giangreco, and Yori Gidron *How Breathing Can Help You Make Better*

Decisions: Two studies on the effects of breathing patterns on heart rate variability and decision making in business cases International Journal of Psychophysiology (first pub'd online: March 1, 2019) DOI: 10.1016/i.iipsycho.2019.02.011

Mitchell, D (2003) Child Development and Pedagogical Issues The Association of Waldorf Schools of North America

McManus, S., Hassiotis, A., Jenkins, R., Dennis, M., Aznar, C., & Appleby, L. (2016). Chapter 12: Suicidal thoughts, suicide attempts, and self-harm. In S., McManus, P., Bebbington, R., Jenkins & T. Brugha (Eds.) Mental health and wellbeing in England: Adult Psychiatric Morbidity Survey 2014 Leeds: NHS Digital

Nahas Z., Marangell L.B., Husain M.M., Rush AJ., Sackeim H.A., Lisanby S.H., et al Two-year outcome of vagus nerve stimulation (VNS) for treatment of major depressive episodes J Clin Psychiatry. 2005;66:1097–104

Peper, E., Pollock, W., Harvey, R., Yoshino, A., Daubenmier, J., & Anziani, M. (2019) Which quiets the mind more quickly and increases HRV: Toning or mindfulness? NeuroRegulation, 6(3), 128–133. https://doi.org/10.15540/nr.6.3.128

Pramanik T, Sharma HO, Mishra S, Mishra A,

Prajapati, R., Singh S.J Altern Immediate effect of pranayama on blood pressure and heart rate 2009 Mar;15(3):293-5. doi: 10.1089/acm.2008.0440

Roderik, J.S., Gerritsen and Guido P.H. Band Breath of Life: The Respiratory Vagal Stimulation Model of Contemplative Activity Frontiers in Human Neuroscience (first pub'd online: October 9, 2018) DOI: 10.3389/fnhum.2018.00397

Rosenthal, R., &. Jacobson, L. (1963) Teachers' expectancies: Determinants of pupils' IQ gains Psychological Reports, 19, 115-118

Stansfeld, S., Clark, C., Bebbington, P., King, M., Jenkins, R., & Hinchliffe, S. (2016) Chapter 2: Common mental disorders In, S., McManus, P., Bebbington, R., Jenkins & T. Brugha (Eds.) Mental health and wellbeing in England: Adult Psychiatric Morbidity Survey 2014 Leeds: NHS Digital

Satir, V., Banmen, J., Gerberm, J., & Gomori, M. (1991) The Satir Model: Family Therapy and Beyond Palo Alto, CA: Science & Behaviour Books Inc.

Samson, Steven Alan (1979) Value System Processing Study Guide Faculty Publications and Presentations. Paper 210. http://digitalcommons.liberty.edu/gov_fac_pubs/210

Further reading

Bandler, R. and Bradstock, G. and Fitzpatrick, O. (2019) *Thinking on Purpose* New Thinking Publications

Bandler, R. and Benson, K. (2016) *Teaching Excellence* BB Publications

Bandler, R. and Thomson, G. (2011) *The Secrets of Being Happy* I.M. Press, Inc

Bandler, R. (2008) *Get The Life You Want* Health Communications Inc. Florida

Bandler, R. and Grinder, J. and Satir, V. (1976) *Changing With Families* Science and Behavior Books, Inc

Becker, R.O. and Selden, G. (1985) *The Body Electric* Harper Collins

Beever, S. (2009) *Happy Kids Happy You* Crown House Publishing Ltd

Brandes, B. (2015) *The Symphony of Reflexes* Quantum Reflex Integration, Inc

Breuning, L.G. (2015) *Habits of a Happy Brain - Retrain Your Brain to Boost Your Serotonin, Dopamine, Oxytocin, & Endorphin Levels* Adams Media

Carter, R. (2009) *The Brain Book* DK, London

Charvet, S.R. (1997) *Words That Change Minds* Kendall/Hunt Publishing Co.

Carlson, R. (1993) *Stop Thinking Start Living* Harper Collins

Demos, J. (2005) *Getting Started With Neurofeedback* Norton & Co

Dispenza, J. (2014) *You are the Placebo - Making your mind matter* Hay House

Eaton, A. (2015) *Words That Work - How to get kids to do almost anything* Matador

Eageman, D. (2015) *The Brain - The Story of You* Cannongate Books. Edinburgh

Green, J.D. and Dilts, R. (1982) *Neuro-Linguistic Programming in Family Therapy, in Family Counseling and Therapy* Horne & Olsen editors, Peacock Publishers, Inc., Itasca, IL

Grinder, J. and Bandler, R. and DeLozier, J. and Dilts, R. (1980) *Neuro-Linguistic Programming - The Study of the Structure of Subjective Experience, Volume I* Meta Publications, Capitola, CA

Hefferon, K (2113) *Positive Psychology and the Body - The somatopsychic side to flourishing* Open University Press

Katz, L. and Rubin, M. (1999) *Keep Your Brain Alive* Workman Publishing Company, New York

Korb, A. (2015) *Upward Spiral: Using Neuroscience to Reverse the Course of Depression, One Small Change at a Time* New Harbinger Publications

Macroy, T.D. (1978) *Linguistic Surface Structures in Family Interaction in Dissertation* Abstracts International, Utah State University Meta Publications, Capitola, CA

McGilchrist, I. (2009) *The Master and his Emissary* Yale University Press

Neill, M. (2007) *Feel Happy Now!* Hay House

Mate, G. (2003) *When The Body Says No - Understanding the Stress-Disease Connection* Ebury Publishing ISBN: 9781785042225

Owen, N. (2006) *The Magic of Metaphor 77 Stories for teachers, trainers & thinkers* Crown House Publishing Ltd

Petitmengin, C. (2006) *Describing one's subjective experience in the second person - An interview method for the science of consciousness* Phenomenology and the Cognitive Sciences 5(3-4): 229-269

Peters, S. (2018) *The Silent Guides* Lagom Publications

Perry, N. and Perry, E. (2018) *Botanical Brain Balms* Filbert Press

Portwood, M (1999) *Developmental Dyspraxia* Fulton Publishers

Porges, S. (2011) *The Polyvagal Theory* W. W Norton & Co.

Thomson, G. and Khan, K. (2008) *Magic In Practice - Introducing Medical NLP* Hammersmith Press, London, UK

Van der Kolk, B. (2014) *The Body Keeps Score -Mind, brain and body in the transformation of trauma* Penguin Books

Walker, L. (2004) *Changing With NLP - A casebook of NLP in medical practice* Radcliffe Medical Press, Oxford

Printed in Great Britain
by Amazon

35654736R00098